D0422900

UNPLUG *and* PLAY

50 ORIGINAL GROUP GAMES *that don't need charging!*

Technology-free fun for groups of all ages. No texting, tweeting, or surfing allowed!

BRAD BERGER

To Taylor and Rebekah

Published by Familius LLC, www.familius.com

Familius books are available at special discounts for bulk purchases, whether for sales promotions or for family or corporate use. For more information, contact Familius Sales at 559-876-2170 or email orders@familius.com.

Library of Congress Cataloging-in-Publication Data
2015955936
Print ISBN 9781942934509
Ebook ISBN 9781944822088

Printed in China

Edited by Brooke Jorden
Cover design by David Miles
Book design by David Miles and Brooke Jorden

10 9 8 7 6 5 4 3 2 1

First Edition

TAKE A BREAK FROM . . .

LOOKING AT THE TOPS OF PEOPLE'S HEADS WHILE THEY TYPE AND CLICK

A FRIEND LOOKING AT SOMETHING ON HIS PHONE THAT MIGHT BE MORE INTERESTING THAN YOU

TEXTING

SOCIAL MEDIA

POSTING PHOTOS, VIDEOS, AND STATUS UPDATES

GAMES INVOLVING LITTLE TO NO COMMUNICATION

EVERYONE PLUGGED INTO THEIR DEVICES DURING GROUP OR FAMILY ACTIVITIES

WHEN TO USE THIS BOOK . . .

GAME NIGHTS

DINNER PARTIES

COCKTAIL PARTIES

BIRTHDAY PARTIES

ANY KIND OF PARTY

FAMILY GATHERINGS

CLASSROOM ACTIVITIES

VACATIONS

HOLIDAYS

ROAD TRIPS

LONG FLIGHTS

SHORT FLIGHTS

BEFORE MEALS

DURING MEALS

AFTER MEALS

ON A BOAT OR CRUISE

IN A LONG LINE AT AN AMUSEMENT PARK

IN A LONG LINE FOR ANYTHING

SHIPWRECKED ON A DESERTED ISLAND

SHIPWRECKED ON A CROWDED ISLAND

TRAPPED IN A LARGE TENT

YOU SHOULD USE THIS BOOK WITH:

YOUR FRIENDS

YOUR FAMILY

YOUR STUDENTS

YOUR COLLEAGUES

YOUR SORORITY SISTERS

YOUR FRATERNITY BROTHERS

YOUR TEAMMATES

YOUR ROOMMATES

YOUR CELL MATES

PRIMATES

VEGETARIANS

MEAT EATERS

PEOPLE YOU LIKE

PEOPLE YOU LOVE

PEOPLE FROM SWEDEN

MOST HOBBITS

YOUR NEIGHBORS

YOUR IN-LAWS

YOUR DOCTORS

YOUR NURSES

YOUR LAWYERS

YOUR ACCOUNTANTS

WIZARDS NAMED TIM

FANS OF THE MOVIE *GIGLI*

OLD PEOPLE AND YOUNG PEOPLE AND ANYONE IN BETWEEN

AUTHOR'S NOTE

Game nights, parties, family gatherings, vacations, road trips, and more! The following games are simply . . . well, fun!

I put this book together for one reason. I play these games with my family and friends, and we always have a blast, so I decided to organize them into a book. This means that (1) my family and I can always refer back without having to remember the games and the rules we put in place and (2) I can share our games with the world. Now keep in mind that the rules and scoring are merely suggestions. Every group of players is different. For instance, some of you are more competitive than others. So be flexible. Make up your own rules if you'd like. You can decide whether to keep score or not. These games can be lots of fun no matter how you play them. The rules are simply there because they have worked for us. You'll understand why as you play them.

The games are organized into six groups:

1. **Matchmaker, Matchmaker** (Match your lists with the lists of the other players.)
2. **Call My Bluff** (Use your creativity, learn a lot more about the players in your group, and see who is best at bluffing.)
3. **That's My Plan, and I'm Sticking to It!** (These games are all about strategy. Come up with the best plan to accomplish your goal.)
4. **Ready, Set, Go!** (Find the answer faster than everyone else.)
5. **Try to Remember** (Test your memory against others.)

6. **I'm Puzzled!** (Create easy-to-make puzzles for group competitions.)

These games are for all ages and all levels. You will decide how to play them based on your own group! For instance, in games that require coming up with categories, the categories you choose will most likely be different with young kids in the game than with adults. A group of engineers may choose different categories or subjects than perhaps a group of Olympic athletes.

Best of all, **PHONES, PADS, PODS, OR ELECTRONIC DEVICES OF ANY KIND ARE NEITHER ALLOWED NOR REQUIRED!** Play these games for fifteen minutes or fifteen hours. Either way, you'll often notice that nobody is texting, tweeting, sending emails, or surfing the web. Everyone is engaged, communicating, and having fun with each other. Go ahead and give them a try! HAVE FUN!

Brad Berger

FYI

RECOMMENDED PLAYERS, PENS AND PAPER/INDEX CARDS

Below the title of each game, you will see a recommended number of players. This is simply a strong suggestion in some cases and an absolute necessity in others.

All you will need to play most of these games are pens (or pencils or markers or something to write with) and paper. Some games don't require anything at all besides the players themselves. For several games, right next to the recommended players suggestion, you will see . That means paper and pens are required. For some of the games, we recommend index cards over paper. You'll understand why as you read the game instructions.

FOUR IMPORTANT TIPS WHEN PLAYING THESE GAMES

1. **Assign a Game Director and Scorekeeper.** The games certainly run more smoothly when you have someone who is the designated organizer.
2. **Make sure you have plenty of paper and writing instruments.** Most of the games in this book require some amount of writing. Ideally, every player should have his own pad or notebook. I like to purchase the small pads you find at many pharmacies and office or school supply stores. Every player puts his name on the pad, and that's his game book for the day, night, or week. It's also a great way to hold on to some of the fun game memories.

3. **BE PATIENT!** Some of these games will take you less than five minutes to figure out. Others will demand slightly more time, and some will require you to read the instructions a few times and to play several practice rounds before your group gets the hang of it. Just stick with it!

4. **No cheating!** Unless, of course, everyone in your group thinks it would be perfectly fine to cheat. Then, by all means, cheat away! Otherwise, for many of these games, you will be on the honor system, depending upon how you decide to keep score. The rules and scoring suggestions have been put in place to make for the best experience with the clear understanding that nobody cheats.

CONTENTS

MATCHMAKER, MATCHMAKER

These matching games are a lot of fun and a great way to get your group quickly into game-playing mode! They always lead to conversations about interests, likes, dislikes, and what each individual in your group considers to be the most popular, common, or well-known choices on many different subjects or themes. In most of the games in this chapter, the objective is simple: match your list with the lists of the other players. Do you think alike?

The first five games in this chapter are similar but NOT the same! Each of these games has a different twist which will greatly influence the choices you make. For these games, you will be asked to come up with your own categories. Many suggestions are provided on the following pages, but the specific categories you select will ultimately be based on the personalities and interests of each individual in your group.

200 SAMPLE CATEGORIES FOR MATCHMAKER GAMES 1-5

1. Popular team sports
2. Popular male first names
3. Popular female first names
4. Popular Olympic sports
5. Popular vegetables

6. Popular fruits
7. The most popular cities people like to visit outside of North America
8. Popular New York City attractions
9. Popular Broadway shows
10. Common things you find in a kitchen
11. Common things you find in a bathroom
12. Popular science fiction movies
13. Popular comedy movies
14. Musical instruments
15. Common types of pasta noodles (not including spaghetti)
16. Things that are green
17. Things that are yellow
18. Things that are red
19. Sports teams with animal names
20. Popular vacation destinations
21. Popular fast food restaurants
22. Popular sports-themed movies
23. Words that begin with the prefixes *prob-*, *prof-*, or *prog-*
24. Common soups served at a restaurant
25. Famous people named Robert or Bob
26. Famous people named Jennifer or Jessica
27. Famous people named John or Joe
28. Popular stores in the mall
29. Popular languages to learn
30. Popular animated movies (past and present)
31. Popular comedians (past and present)

32. Popular breakfast cereals
33. The most popular rock bands of all time
34. Famous painters
35. Popular magazines
36. Famous female singers
37. Famous male singers
38. Famous world leaders (past and present)
39. Things people buy at a hardware store
40. Things people buy most at a supermarket
41. Popular board games
42. Popular automobile manufacturers
43. Things that smell bad
44. Things that smell great
45. Famous actors, actresses, singers, or athletes who have gotten themselves into trouble
46. People who have made the biggest impact on the world in the past 100 years (positive or negative)
47. Popular TV dramas
48. Popular TV comedies
49. Songs with the word *love* in the title
50. The world's most well-known large corporations
51. Popular horror films
52. Popular Disney characters
53. Things that are sharp (not including a knife)
54. Common sports injuries
55. Cities in the world that begin with the letter *S*
56. Cities in the world that begin with the letter *M*
57. Common foods at a barbecue
58. Hollywood male actors many people consider to be good looking

59. Popular authors
60. Popular house pets (not including dogs or cats)
61. Common things found in a garage
62. Popular exercise routines
63. Common restaurant chains
64. Types of balls
65. Types of dressings
66. Herbs or spices
67. Popular ways to eat chicken (or specific chicken dishes)
68. Types of fish
69. Words or phrases many English speakers know in other languages
70. Popular zoo animals
71. Words that rhyme with *dark*
72. Things that are hot
73. Things that are cold
74. Movies that have won Oscars
75. Famous basketball players
76. Famous baseball players
77. Famous football players
78. The world's greatest inventions
79. Well-known shoe brands
80. Well-known brands of beer
81. Common brands of chocolate bars
82. Popular desserts ordered in a restaurant
83. Popular ice cream flavors
84. Famous stadiums, arenas, or concert halls
85. Things that are scary

86. Types of breads
87. The most popular types of cookies
88. Things people spend money on
89. Psychological thriller movies
90. Popular reality TV shows
91. Common illnesses
92. Popular TV show hosts
93. Popular kinds of sandwiches
94. Popular male actors of all time no longer living
95. Popular female actresses of all time no longer living
96. Things that break
97. Things you wear
98. Common snacks
99. Countries with the hottest climates
100. Common park activities
101. Famous people named Michael or Matt
102. Hotel chains
103. Popular Muppets
104. Types of pies
105. Casino games
106. Famous actors who were *Saturday Night Live* cast members
107. Common professions
108. Well-known rivers, seas, or lakes
109. Countries in Africa
110. Popular movies with sequels
111. Famous superheroes
112. Water activities
113. Things people do while wearing a helmet

114. Famous presidents

115. The highest-grossing movies of all time

116. Popular games played indoors

117. Popular cable TV channels

118. Frequently used words that begin with the letter *q*

119. Frequently used words that begin with the letter *z*

120. Adjectives used to describe people in a positive way

121. Adjectives used to describe people in a negative way

122. Famous people who became famous when they were kids

123. Common street signs

124. Popular American sports teams

125. Cities or countries that begin with the letter *C*

126. Actors who play tough guys in movies

127. Activities or sports you probably shouldn't do naked

128. Things people do before they go to bed

129. Common words with a silent *k* or *b*

130. Well-known Canadian cities

131. The most well-known dance styles

132. Things you open, turn on, or start

133. Types of juices

134. Words that begin with *wh-*

135. Popular individual (as opposed to team) sports

136. Well-known bugs and insects

137. Dangerous sports

138. Types of street signs

139. Common texting abbreviations
140. Well-known universities
141. Places where people wait in long lines
142. Cities or countries that begin with the letter *P*
143. The most popular cheeses
144. Types of salads
145. Weather terms (not including *cold* or *hot*)
146. Common words or phrases used by announcers at a baseball game
147. Famous blonde celebrities
148. Things you would find at a gym
149. The most famous country singers of all time
150. Types of cakes
151. Specific foods or dishes that are really messy to eat
152. Names people give their pet dogs and cats
153. Common names for streets in the United States
154. The most popular TV shows ever about solving crimes
155. Popular western movies
156. Wealthy people in the world
157. Successful college sports teams
158. Top brands of soda (pop) not including Coke and Pepsi
159. Common allergies
160. Hollywood actresses many people consider to be good looking
161. World cities or regions that have had major historical events occur in the last 100 years
162. Movies or TV shows starring or about an animal or animals

163. Popular card games

164. Hotels with casinos

165. Famous brothers, sisters, fathers and sons, or mothers and daughters

166. Uniform numbers of famous athletes

167. Specific vacation destinations with beautiful beaches

168. Popular US cities to visit (not including New York, Chicago, or LA)

169. Popular European cities to visit that are not in France, Italy, or the UK

170. Famous people named Bill or William

171. Popular romance movies

172. Popular cities or towns for skiing

173. The greatest tennis players of all time (male or female)

174. Famous fashion designers

175. Special days/holidays mentioned on a calendar in the United States

176. Popular salad dressings

177. Popular sauces

178. Common items used for cleaning

179. Popular singers/musicians who have acted in movies

180. Popular companies/brands associated with technology

181. Popular game shows

182. Popular TV shows before 1980

183. The most popular video games of all time

184. Well-known actors/actresses who have played animated characters in movies

185. Famous movie directors

186. Countries with large populations (not including China)

187. Things people collect

188. US cities with only one or two professional teams in the four major US sports

189. Cities that have hosted the Olympics

190. Reasons kids get into trouble at school

191. Well-known movie villains

192. Popular dog breeds

193. Frequently used three-letter words in the English language

194. Common last names in the United States

195. The most recognizable buildings in the world

196. Popular brands of cleaning products

197. Well-known chemical elements

198. Famous celebrity couples

199. Famous actor pairs who have worked together in more than one movie

200. Popular college degrees

CATEGORIES NOT RECOMMENDED FOR MATCHMAKER GAMES 1–5

1. Famous people named Charlize
2. Things you do when locked in a closet
3. Really friendly cannibals
4. Good-looking men with nose rings
5. Well-known tall couples who are afraid of heights
6. What your dog thinks when you leave the house
7. Songs about Roxanne or Levon
8. Conservative drag queens
9. People in your group with bad breath
10. Things vampires do in their spare time (vampire hobbies)

POPULAR

DO YOU HAVE A PULSE ON POPULAR OPINION?

PREPARATION

Each player comes up with five categories that will lead to many possible answers (see pages 1–9 for ideas) and places them in a hat or facedown on a table mixed in with all of the others.

OBJECTIVE

A player's goal is to match his or her selections with as many of the other players' selections as possible in every chosen category. When a category is selected, players list the items that they think will be the most popular choices, meaning the items in a given category they predict will be on most of the lists of the players in the group. The more players a person matches for each of his or her selections, the more points he or she earns.

GAME TIME

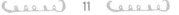

Players take turns drawing categories out of the hat without looking. Once Player 1 selects a random category for the first round, he decides how many items (from five to ten) everyone will list in that category.

TIP: On your turn, if you feel you can list a lot of items in your category, pick a high number, giving yourself the chance to earn more points than other players in the game who aren't as knowledgeable about that category.

Once the category is announced, no players may speak until all players have completed their lists. Allow players two minutes to create their lists. If a player cannot finish his or her list in that time, that player will have fewer chances to score points.

IMPORTANT: Players may not list more items than the number required!

Once every player has read and/or received points for all listed items, each player gives his or her total points for the round to the scorekeeper, and play continues as Player 2 draws a new category. If you pick a category from the hat that was evidently submitted by more than one person and has already been used, pick again.

SCORING

Once all players have completed their lists, players take turns going around the room announcing items they have listed one at a time. Players earn 1 point for every person who matched one of their items—including a point for themselves. (For example, if a player matches an item on his or her list with three other players, all four players receive 4 points for that item.) Add up the points for each item to determine the total for that category. Players receive no points for an item if they were the only one who listed it.

NOTE: There is no need to repeat an item that has been said by another player since everyone already has a point total for that item.

EXAMPLE

Let's say you have a game of seven players. Player 1 goes first and randomly selects from the hat the category *Things that are green*. He then decides that he wants everyone to list eight things that are green. Players have two minutes to list their eight items.

NOTE: If you can't come up with eight, then you simply will have fewer chances to score in the round than those who have eight listed. It certainly doesn't mean you won't get a high score, but, ideally, you want to give yourself the best chance by listing the maximum number of items requested.

After every player writes down eight items that are green, players take turns reading the items on their lists. Player 1 goes first. If his first item is *broccoli* and five out of the seven players (including Player 1) had *broccoli* on their lists, then all five of those players receive 5 points (1 point per player). The other two players receive nothing.

Player 2 goes next and reads one of her items. If that item is *grass* and three of the seven players said *grass*, then those three get 3 points for *grass*. Player 3 then reads one of his items, and so on until every player reads all eight of his or her green things.

Again, no points are awarded if only one player has a specific item. In other words, if Player 4 has *traffic light* on her list and nobody else wrote *traffic light*, Player 4 would not get any points for that item. If one other player had *traffic light*, he and Player 4 would both get 2 points.

MATCH JACK

HOW WELL CAN YOU MATCH YOUR SELECTIONS WITH ANOTHER PLAYER IN YOUR GROUP?

PREPARATION

Each player comes up with five categories that will lead to many possible answers (see pages 1–9 for ideas) and places them in a hat or facedown on a table mixed in with all of the others.

OBJECTIVE

The objective is to list items that will match with the items on the list of ONE SPECIFIC PLAYER—the player who randomly picks the category in each round.

GAME TIME

Player 1 picks a random category from the hat and reads it aloud. All players have two minutes to make a list of as many items in that category as possible that will match with the list of Player 1 (up to ten items).

NOTE: It is important for Player 1 to list as many items as possible (up to ten) on his turn in order to earn as many points as possible. More on that under "Scoring."

When two minutes are up, Player 1 announces how many items he has on his list. The rest of the players must narrow their lists down to the same number (or less, if they don't have as many) as Player 1. You cannot have any more listed than Player 1 has.

When all players' items have been compared to Player 1's list, all of the players, including Player 1, add up the points they earned for Player 1's round (see "Scoring"). Player 2 then picks a new random category for her round, and so on. If you pick a category from the hat that was evidently submitted by more than one person and has already been used, pick again.

EXAMPLE

Player 1 goes first and picks *Popular Olympic Sports* out of the hat. When two minutes are up, Player 1 announces that he has eight items listed. Every player must now make sure they have no more than eight popular Olympic sports on their lists. So if Player 2 had 10 items on her list, she must CROSS OUT two of them. Once everyone is done finalizing their lists of eight, Player 1 reveals his eight items.

SCORING

Points are awarded based on the number of matched items. Player 1 (or whichever player chose the category) receives 4 points for each correct match with every other player in the game. All other players receive 10 points for every item they matched on the list of the player who selected the category. For instance, in the above example with *Popular Olympic sports*, everyone had to match with Player 1. If Player 3 matched six items correctly with Player 1, Player 3 would get 60 points and Player 1 would get 24 points. If Player 5 matched four items correctly with Player 1, Player 5 would get 40 points and Player 1 would get 16 points. At the same time, Player 1 would be adding up the points he earned from each other player for his grand total on that round.

SAMPLE:

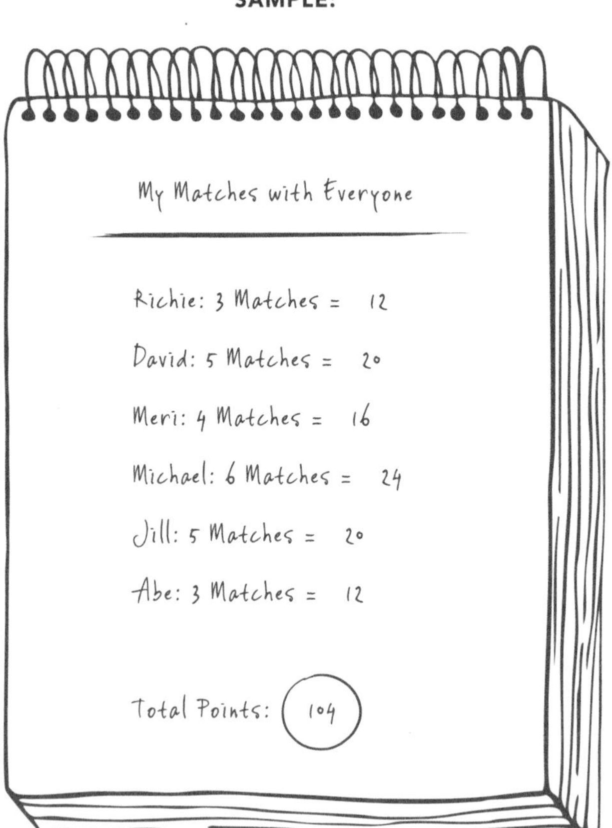

My Matches with Everyone
Richie: 3 Matches = 12
David: 5 Matches = 20
Meri: 4 Matches = 16
Michael: 6 Matches = 24
Jill: 5 Matches = 20
Abe: 3 Matches = 12
Total Points: 104

I CHALLENGE

ARE YOU AND YOUR PARTNER UP FOR THE CHALLENGE?

PREPARATION

Each player comes up with five categories that will lead to many possible answers (see pages 1–9 for ideas) and places them in a hat or facedown on a table mixed in with all of the others.

Player 1 begins by randomly picking a certain number of categories out of the hat. That number is determined by dividing the number of players in the game by two. (For instance, if there are six players in the game, Player 1 would pick out three categories.) If there is an odd number of players in the game, then round down. (In other words, with nine players, round down to eight and pick out four categories.) Player 1 flips over the categories for everyone to see and then determines which two players he is going to challenge in each category.

> **NOTE:** Player 1 has a distinct advantage in his round: he gets to select his partner and their category first. Player 1 then pairs up the remaining players and assigns each pair one of the remaining categories. If there are an odd number of players in the game, one player (call

him the "extra player") will not be paired up initially in each round, but he will still contribute and earn or lose points in the round like everyone else. (More on that under "With an Odd Number of Players.")

OBJECTIVE

Once categories and pairs have been chosen, each player must attempt to match the items related to the category on his list with the items on his partner's list.

GAME TIME

With categories assigned, all pairs begin making their lists at the same time. Both players in each pairing must write down a total of three items each. Once the selection of categories begins, no talking is allowed amongst the players trying to match until every player is finished making his list. Once everyone is finished making their lists, scoring begins.

SCORING

If a pair gets at least two matches in their category, each player in the pair earns 5 points. If a pair gets less than two matches, everyone else in the game earns 5 points for their lack of success. If a pair gets all three to match, they get 20 points each.

EXAMPLE

Let's say you have a game of six players. Player 1 goes first and picks out three random categories: *Common board games*, *Popular stores in the mall*, and *Famous people named Bill or William*. First, he decides who in the round should be his partner and which of these three categories will be easiest for them to match. Let's say he chooses Player 2 as his partner and *Common board games* as their category. He then decides which pairs of players will have the most difficulty matching their lists for the *Popular stores in the mall* and *Famous people named Bill or William* categories.

He assigns Players 3 and 5 and Players 4 and 6 to be partners, and all pairs begin making their lists according to their assigned categories. Player 1 and Player 2 try to predict which board games the other will put on his list.

WITH AN ODD NUMBER OF PLAYERS

Once the teams are determined, the extra player who was not selected by Player 1 for a team for the round decides who in the game she wants to help. She can help only one person in the game try to match with his partner. She can choose anyone she likes, and if the team is successful, she will receive the same amount of points as the people on the team she helps. Therefore, in most cases, she will choose to help a player on the team which she feels has the greatest potential to match all three.

SAMPLE TEAMS:

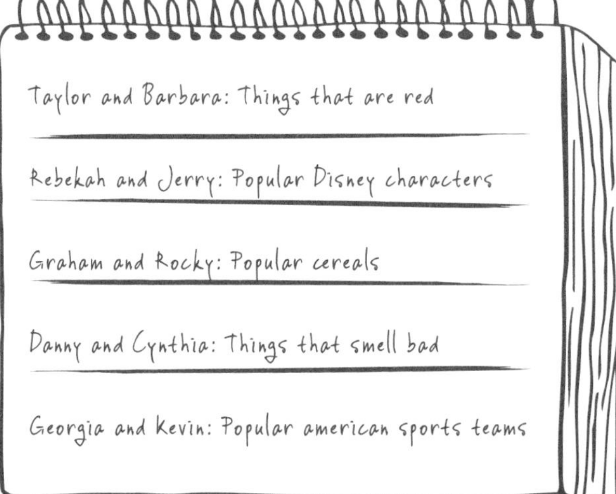

Taylor and Barbara: Things that are red
Rebekah and Jerry: Popular Disney characters
Graham and Rocky: Popular cereals
Danny and Cynthia: Things that smell bad
Georgia and Kevin: Popular american sports teams

PLACE YOUR BETS

HOW CONFIDENT ARE YOU IN EACH OF YOUR SELECTIONS?

PREPARATION

Each player comes up with five categories that will lead to many possible answers (see pages 1–9 for ideas) and places them in a hat or facedown on a table mixed in with all of the others.

OBJECTIVE

Players earn points based on how confident they are in each of their items showing up on the majority of the lists of the other players in the game.

GAME TIME

Player 1 picks a random category from the hat and reads it aloud. Once a category is selected, each player has up to two minutes to make his or her list and there is no talking until everyone is done. Each player lists a total of five items related to that category. The five items should be placed on the list in order of confidence. The first selection should be the one a player is positive will be listed by most players, and the last selection should be the one a player is least positive about most players including on their lists. If for any reason a player cannot come up with five items in a given category, the ordering will remain the same, but he or she will have fewer chances to score.

When time is up, players take turns reading items on their lists, beginning with the selections placed by everyone in the number 5 position and ending with the selections placed by everyone in the number 1 position. Players keep track of the points earned at each level (see "Scoring").

Play continues as players take turns picking out categories, listing five items for each category and adding up their scores in each round.

SCORING

In order to get points for each selection, players' choices must match with MORE THAN HALF of the players in the game. A player's number 1 selection, when matched with more than half of the players, earns 10 points. The number 2 selection earns 8 points; number 3 earns 6 points; number 4 earns 4 points; and number 5 earns 2 points. Again, if a player does not have five items listed, he or she will not be able to earn points for the missing lower levels.

IMPORTANT: You receive NO POINTS for an item on your list that isn't listed by more than half of the players in your group!

EXAMPLE

Say the first category chosen was *Popular comedians* and Player 1 put *Chris Rock* first on his list. If more than half of the total players in the game had Chris Rock anywhere on their lists, Player 1 would receive 10 points. However, not everyone who had Chris Rock would necessarily get 10 points. If one of those players put Chris Rock as number 3, that player would only get 6 points. If another player put Chris Rock as number 5, that player would only get 2 points. If only half or less than half of the players in the game had Chris Rock, then nobody would get points for that comedian.

THE BONUS SIDE BET OPTION

This is an important and rather fun addition to this game. Once players have decided on their list of five selections in the category, they may choose to make some bonus selections and decide to place additional bets on those. A bonus selection is an item a player did NOT put on his or her list that the player believes is probably on ONE of the other players' lists of five.

For example, with the "Popular comedians" category above, if Player 2 strongly feels that ONE person in her group would put down Jay Leno as one of their top five (AND ONLY ONE!), then she may make a side bet on her page of up to 20 points that it will happen. If she bet 4 points that Jay Leno would be on just ONE of the other player's top five and she was right, she would earn an additional 4 points in that round. However, if nobody or more than one person in the group had Jay Leno in their list of five, then Player 2 would lose the points she wagered!

> **IMPORTANT:** You may bet on as many additional items for each category as you'd like, but you may not total more than 20 points in your combined side bets. You will reveal the results of your side bets after all players have read their top five lists.

SAMPLE:

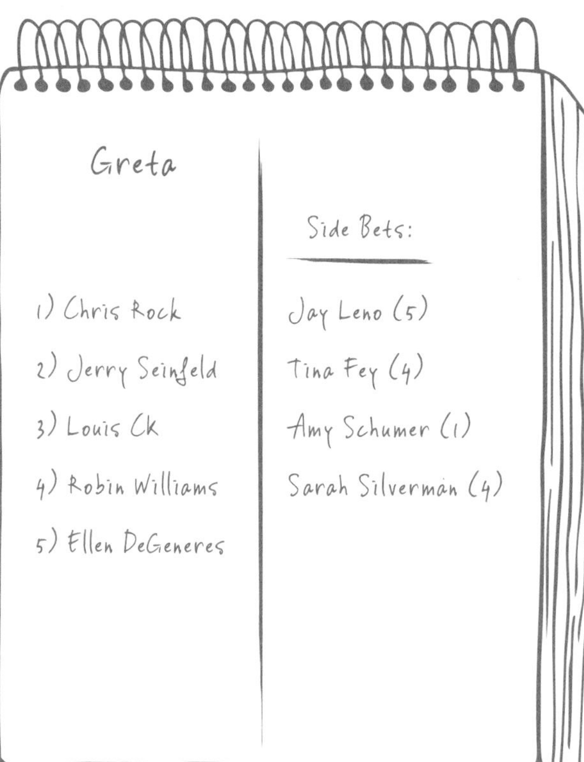
Greta
1) Chris Rock
2) Jerry Seinfeld
3) Louis Ck
4) Robin Williams
5) Ellen DeGeneres
Side Bets:
Jay Leno (5)
Tina Fey (4)
Amy Schumer (1)
Sarah Silverman (4)

NOBODY HAD THAT!

FOOL YOUR FRIENDS INTO THINKING YOUR ITEM WAS ON ONE OF THEIR LISTS.

PREPARATION

Each player comes up with five categories that will lead to many possible answers (see pages 1–9 for ideas) and places them in a hat or facedown on a table mixed in with all of the others.

OBJECTIVE

For each selected category in this game, one player chooses a total of three items from all of the other players' lists that he or she feels most people would think that nobody actually said. That player must also come up with one item that most people would believe was on one of the player's lists. All the other players must try to determine which item was added by the player leading the round.

GAME TIME

Play begins with every player randomly selecting one category each from the hat. Player 1 announces his category first. All players then write down three items related to that category that they believe other players will write as well. Players write these items on two pieces of paper: (1) a small piece that they will hand to Player 1 (Make them legible so Player 1 has no trouble reading any of them!) and (2) a separate sheet to keep track of their responses. On this second sheet, players should write *Player 1* (or the player who chose the category) at the top. Also on the extra sheet of paper, under the list of three items, write *Nobody* and leave a blank space next to it to be filled in later.

Player 1 keeps all of the lists of items for his category together in a pile and puts the pile aside. Nobody should be able to see the lists—Player 1 must keep them hidden.

Player 2 then announces the category she picked. Everyone must then make a list of three popular items for Player 2's category and hand them over to Player 2. Again, write the three popular items you chose for Player 2 next to her name and category on your separate page with the items you chose for Player 1, and again place the word *Nobody* right under that list with a space next to it.

Repeat this process for every player in the game until everyone hands their lists to the final player. Now everyone looks at the lists they were provided from the other players, and each player must now make a very important decision at the same time!

Each player looks at all of the lists for his or her category. He or she then selects three items from the combined lists from all of the other players and ADDS ONE MORE ITEM that wasn't on anyone else's list. Once all players have finished this task, Player 1 goes first.

Player 1 reads his list of four in a random order, and the other players must guess which one is the one from Player 1—the one nobody had! Players write down their guesses next to the word *Nobody* under the lists made for Player 1's category.

Once each player writes his or her guess under Player 1's column, everyone puts down their pen (no changing responses once pens are down) and tells Player 1 what item they chose as the one nobody had. Player 1 then reveals who was correct and hands out points.

Player 2 then reveals her list of four items for her category, and everyone makes their guesses as to which item Player 2 added . . . and so on until all guesses for each category are made.

SCORING

Player 1 receives 4 points for every player who doesn't pick the item he added. Every player who guessed the item nobody had (the item Player 1 added) correctly will multiply the number of players who got it right by 3, and that is each player's point total. Finally, players LOSE 5 POINTS for every player who chooses one of THEIR ITEMS as the one nobody had on their lists!

So, for example, with seven total players, let's say Player 1 fools four people. Player 1 receives 16 points (4 X 4). This means two of the other players guessed correctly. Those two players earn 6 points each (2 X 3).

In addition, if two of the four players Player 1 fooled guessed an item from Player 6 as the item nobody had, Player 6 loses 10 points. If one player guessed an item from Player 4 was the one nobody had, Player 4 loses 5 points.

> **TIP:** When you announce your category and everyone is making their list of three items, YOU should make your own list of as many items as you can think of in the category. This way, you will hopefully have some good choices of popular items to place on your list that nobody had. It also makes the process quicker when you are later deciding on your list of four.

IMPORTANT: You don't want anyone to guess YOUR item as the one NOBODY HAD! So when making your lists in each category, you will probably want to put the most obvious choices each time so the player making the decision doesn't include any of your items on his or her list of four. You don't want the player who selected the category to score a lot of points on his or her turn, and you certainly don't want to lose points by having an item other players think wasn't on anyone's list.

EXAMPLE

Let's say Player 1 picks the category *Famous horror films*. Everyone except Player 1 writes down three famous horror films and hands them to Player 1 without letting anyone else see them. These three famous horror films should be the most popular each player can think of! Now, a lot of horror films are listed. Films such as *Psycho, Halloween, The Exorcist, A Nightmare on Elm Street*, etc., come up. However, nobody puts *The Shining*! So Player 1 decides to make *The Shining* the one he adds—the one nobody had! He figures people in the game would feel at least one person wrote down *The Shining*. Player 1 also sees movies such as *Alien, Scream*, and *The Blair Witch Project*, and only one person had each of those. Since only one person had each and he feels those movies are not as mainstream as the other entries, he decides to mix those three in with *The Shining* for his final list of four.

He reads his list in any order, and everyone makes their guesses. Points are distributed as mentioned above, and Player 2 announces her list of four that she selected for her category.

WHAT WOULD MOST PEOPLE SAY?

MAKE IT DIFFICULT FOR EVERYONE TO CHOOSE FROM THREE GREAT OPTIONS!

PREPARATION

Each player comes up with a multiple-choice question and three specific, equally popular answers. Possible questions might sound like these: "If you could only have one type of food for the rest of your life, what would it be: (A) Italian, (B) Chinese, or (C) sushi?" Or "Which of these three vacation options would be your first choice: (A) Hawaii, (B) an African safari, or (C) Paris?"

OBJECTIVE

The player leading each round must come up with a question and three answers that will make it difficult for the other players in the game to determine the obvious popular choice, while the other players try to guess the most popular choices for everyone else's questions.

GAME TIME

Starting with Player 1, all players take turns revealing their multiple-choice questions and answers. Each player in the game (including the player who came up with the question) then silently writes down the answer he or she thinks most people would say.

> **IMPORTANT:** Note that your answer isn't necessarily what YOU would say. Try to predict what you think MOST people would say—people in general, but more importantly, the people in the game! Of course, as with most games in this book, never let anyone see your answers until they are all revealed—and do not peek!

Once Player 1 has posed his question and all answers have been written down, all players reveal their answers. The person who asks each question should keep track of how many people voted for each possible answer. When all the answers are revealed, tally the scores for that question. Play continues as Player 2 asks her question, and so on until all players have had a chance to ask their questions.

SCORING

Each player (including the player who wrote each question) gets one point for each matched answer. You don't get any points if you are the only one who picked a specific answer, and you don't get any points for YOUR OWN question if everyone in the game picks the same answer! However, all the other players will receive points equal to the number of matches, including the question-asker's answer.

The player who asked the question has the opportunity to earn bonus points. The number of bonus points is equal to the number of players in the game. If no single answer from the three possibilities was chosen by MORE THAN HALF of the players, the player who asked the question gets the bonus points.

> **IMPORTANT:** These bonus points can give a real advantage in the game, so when you write your question, be sure that your three options are all equally popular rather than having one overwhelmingly obvious choice that might lead more than half the players to choose it.

At the end of the game—whether after one round or multiple rounds with different questions from each player—the player with the most points wins.

EXAMPLE

Let's say there are six players in the game. Player 1 asks, "If you could only have one type of food for the rest of your life, what would it be: (A) Italian, (B) Chinese, or (C) sushi?" Everyone reveals their answers at once, holding up a paper that says *A*, *B*, or *C*. Three players chose Chinese, two players chose Italian, and one chose sushi. Player 1 earns 6 bonus points because NONE of the three possible food choices was chosen by MORE THAN HALF (in this case, more than three) of the players. The players who chose Chinese each earned 3 points; the players who chose Italian each earned 2 points; the player who chose sushi did not earn any points because he did not match with anyone. After the scores are tallied, the game moves on to Player 2's question. She asks, "Which of these three vacation options would be your first choice: (A) Hawaii, (B) an African safari, or (C) Paris?" All six players put down *Hawaii*, so the five other players each earn 6 points but Player 2 earns no points because all six players in the game picked the same answer.

GREAT MINDS THINK ALIKE

WHICH PEOPLE IN YOUR GROUP ARE THE MOST CONNECTED?

PREPARATION

Every player in the game must make a grid of five rows across and five columns down for a total of twenty-five boxes. Number the boxes from 1 to 25 going horizontally across the top row, then down to the second, and so on. In the end, the number 1 should be in the upper left-hand corner, the number 5 in the upper right-hand corner, the number 21 in the bottom left-hand corner, and the number 25 in the bottom right-hand corner.

On a separate piece of paper, write each player's name (except your own), leaving enough space next to each name for tally marks.

OBJECTIVE

For each of twenty-five random words, players must guess the most popular word that comes to everyone's mind each time. If players connect well with most of the other players in the group, they will have a good chance of being part of the winning couple or team.

GAME TIME

Play begins with Player 1 saying a random word. (Any word goes; just make sure it is a real word and nothing that is a private joke between two of the people in the game.) Let's say Player 1 says "pepper." In box number 1, each player (including Player 1) writes a word he or she thinks everyone else will say after hearing "pepper." Often, that word may simply be the first word that comes to mind. Do not let anyone see your answer! Then Player 2 says a different, randomly chosen word, and in box number 2, all players write a word associated with that word. Play continues until all twenty-five boxes are complete. (It is not necessary for all players to have an equal number of turns coming up with a word for the group.)

Once all twenty-five boxes are filled in, all players reveal their answers to each box one by one, starting with box number 1, and players will start to see which players are on the same mental wavelength.

SCORING

In the end, players will see how well they matched with each individual player in the game on all twenty-five answers by tallying matches. The couple with the most matches wins.

EXAMPLE

For instance, for the word *pepper*, it is reasonable to think many people might write *salt*. If Player 1 wrote *salt* and two other people in the game also wrote *salt*, then Player 1 puts a tally mark next to those players' names on his list. With these two people, Player 1 already has one match each. Everyone does the same with their answers. For box number 2, Player 2 chose "army." If four players wrote *navy*, those four would put tally marks next to the other three players they matched.

TIP: Words like *pepper* and *army* may create a lot of matching. Your words certainly don't have to be that easy. It's really up to each individual player to choose his own word each time it is his turn.

If, at the end of the game, Player 2 and Player 6 matched nine answers out of the twenty-five and no two other players matched as many, they win. Credit can also be given to second and third place couples.

IMPORTANT: In the event of a tie for first place after twenty-five words, simply add another row of boxes and five more words. Everyone competes in the extra round, and the couples in third or fourth place now have the chance to catch up and perhaps win! (These added rows can really heighten the competition because now most players know who they need to match in order to win.) Keep adding one row at a time until a winning couple is revealed once the matches for the last word in the row are determined.

TEAM PLAY OPTION

It can become difficult to keep track of everyone you match for each word with a lot of players, so we recommend following the "Team Play" option if there are more than five players in the game. With team play, you are all still rotating around the room and using the same twenty-five words just like with individual play. The difference is that the scoring becomes a point system.

Teams of three or four players try to match each other rather than the group. In a team of three players, your team receives 2 points if two of you match on a word and 3 points if all three of your answers match.

A team of four players can also earn 2 points if only two of the team members in the group match on a word. However, a team of four players CANNOT earn 3 points! Even if three of the four players match on a word, they still only earn 2 points! Instead, a team of four players has the chance to earn 4 points (1) if all four players' answers match on a word OR (2) if two team members match on the same word and the other two members match on the same word. (For example, if the initial word was *ice* and two people on the team of four wrote *cold* and the other two wrote *cube*, then your team would earn 4 points.)

> **NOTE:** This rule is put in place to make it fairer for teams of three players to compete against teams of four players. Teams of four simply have an advantage over teams of three since they have more opportunities for matches. Therefore, this adjusted scoring slightly removes the advantage.

SAMPLE:

1 cube
2 moon
3 green
4 ball
5 chocolate
6 winter
7 hockey
8 orange
9 foot
10 wave
11 jaws
12 city
13 holiday
14 food
15 Halloween
16 Spain
17 spoon
18 sweet
19 drive
20 frame
21 tennis
22 casino
23 lava
24 Christmas
25 cat
Jennifer ✓✓✓✓✓
Mike ✓✓✓✓✓✓✓
Debbie ✓✓✓✓✓✓✓✓✓
Louis ✓✓✓✓✓✓
Rachel ✓✓✓✓✓✓
Greg ✓✓✓✓✓✓✓✓✓
Phil ✓✓✓✓
Megan ✓✓✓✓✓✓✓✓

FISHING FOR COUPLES

A RACE TO FIND THE RIGHT MATCHES!

PREPARATION

Each player must come up with a group of "couples." What is a couple? For this game, a couple is any two people or things that are somehow connected. You can use actual couples like Napoleon and Josephine, Charles and Diana, or Bill and Hillary. Or you can go with Patrick Swayze and Demi Moore from the movie *Ghost*, Robert Redford and Paul Newman from any number of movies they did together, or Michael Jordan and Scottie Pippin, who played together for the Chicago Bulls. In addition to pairing up well-known people who have some kind of connection, you can go in an entirely different direction and choose pairings like cheddar and swiss, bowl and spoon, chicken noodle and minestrone, spaghetti and linguini, or strawberries and cream.

NOTE: When creating couples, anything goes, as long as you can draw a definite connection. The more creative you are in this game, the more challenging and fun it will be for the players involved.

On index cards or small, evenly shaped pieces of paper, players create the game cards for each round of the game. Each player needs one notecard for every player in the game. (If there are an odd number of players, round down.) The couples will be split between two cards, so divide the total number of players in the game by two to see how many couples each player needs to create.

Each card will contain one part of one couple and will be a game piece for a different player in the game.

Write one part of a couple on one card and the other part of the couple on another card until there is one half of a couple written on each card. Don't let anyone see what you write on any of the cards! In addition, write your name at the bottom of each card on the same side as the item so the player who gets the card knows who the item is from. Once you have created your game cards, mix them up and hand one card out to every player.

NOTE: With an odd number of players in the game, everyone will have one of your cards except you! With an even number of total players in the game, each player will have to keep one of his or her own cards. (For example, with seven total players, every player will have a total of six game cards, one from every other player in the game. With six total players, every player will also have a total of six game cards, but one of those cards will be your own.)

OBJECTIVE

Players attempt to find more matches than everyone else in the game.

GAME TIME

Everyone looks at the cards given to them.

> **IMPORTANT:** Do not let anyone see any of your cards!

Play begins with Player 1 asking if anyone has a specific person or thing that he feels is a match for one of his items. For example, if one of his cards is *bat* and it is from Dianne, he might say, "Does anyone have Dianne's *ball*?" He must say the name of the person as well as the item he thinks may be out there as a match. The reason for this is because it is possible someone else in the game may also have the same card as part of a different couple (in this case, *ball*) and you don't want two people acknowledging that they have the item. In this case, if Player 2 says, "Yes, I have Dianne's ball," then Player 2 must hand the *ball* game card over to Player 1 and Player 1 must show it to Dianne to confirm the match, just in case Dianne has something else matching with *bat*.

> **NOTE:** Players shouldn't say their own item out loud! You never want to reveal what you have to the whole group until the match is confirmed. In this case, if Player 1 says out loud that he has *bat* and Dianne says that it WASN'T the right match, now the rest of the group knows Player 1 has *bat* and someone will most likely easily take the match.

Then Player 2 (seated to the left of Player 1) goes and tries to find a match for one of her cards. If Player 2 says a word and nobody answers, then Player 2 has one strike and must try again when her turn comes the next time. Play continues to rotate to the left, and each player takes a turn trying to find a match for one of his or her items. If a player gets three strikes in a row (meaning on each consecutive turn for three turns), that player must immediately pass one of his or her cards to the player to the right. The player to the right now has another game card to try to match! After a player gives a card to the player to the right, the player who gave away a card starts fresh with another three strikes before he or she has to do that again.

IMPORTANT: Keep in mind that if there are an even number of players in the game, every player will be holding one of his or her own cards at the beginning of the game. You may not ask for a match for your own card since you know what the match is. Therefore, since you are unable to score with your own card, you should be ready to give that card away as soon as you have three strikes against you.

NOTE: The card you are given after a three-strike run may actually already be a match with one of your existing cards, and you can therefore get confirmation on the match from the player who created the couple once your turn comes around again. If you have a confirmed match, place both cards in your match pile, and your turn is over.

SCORING

Eventually, all of the matches will be paired. The number of match cards you end up with is your total points for the round. The player with the most points wins!

TIP: It is recommended that you do not make your couples too difficult or too easy. Something in between always makes this game more interesting! You can also make them tricky by providing items in your group of couples that may match with more than one of your items. For example, with the word *bat*, the true match could have been *glove* and the actual match for *ball* may have been *basket*.

EXAMPLE

Let's say one of Player 1's items is *bat*, and he asks, "Does anyone have Dianne's *ball*?" If *ball* was the actual match for bat (confirmed by Dianne, who submitted both), then Player 2, who had *ball*, must give her card to Player 1, who now has one match! Player 1 just earned two points for the match, and the other player has one less item to match for points. If *ball* wasn't correct, that means *ball* and *bat* are obviously matches for other items in the game, and now everyone knows the word *ball* is out there and exactly who has it! Nobody is certain what Player 1 has on his card other than Player 1 and Dianne since it wasn't revealed. You can only take an educated guess, and that may give someone an important clue about a potential match.

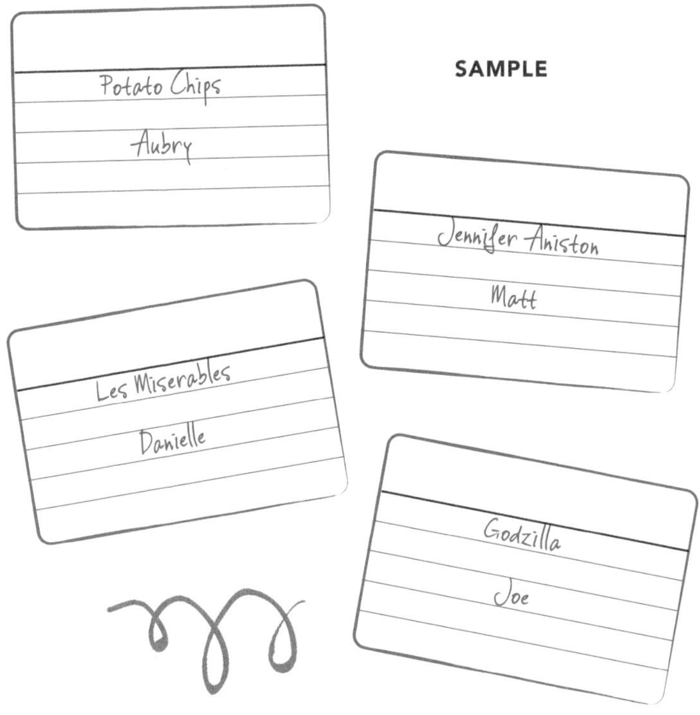

HOW WELL DO THE OTHER PLAYERS KNOW YOU?

Be prepared for laughter and plenty of revelations about each individual and the other players' perception of you!

> **NOTE:** This game can only be played if there are no complete strangers to your group participating. It is mostly for those groups of people who know each other at least fairly well . . . like friends and family members.

PREPARATION

First, write the name of every player in your group on a separate piece of paper. Fold each one and place them all in a hat or facedown on a table. Next, each player must come up with an activity he or she thinks would typically not be associated with or attempted by a member of the group—for example, activities such as "nude sunbathing" or "eating bugs" or "hiking to the top of the tallest mountain in the world" or "walking on fire" or "crashing a wedding" or "entering a hot dog–eating contest." (Some of these activities may not be a big deal for certain members of your group, so be creative and come up with activities that will be out of the norm for your specific group.)

OBJECTIVE

Players must predict the group's consensus about the tendencies and willingness of each individual to engage in certain activities.

GAME TIME

Once everyone has thought of the activity they wish to present, Player 1 announces his activity. Then Player 1 picks two random names from the hat and reveals them. Every player then writes down the activity and lists three people next to it. The first is the person in the group each player thinks is "most likely" to engage in the activity. The second is the person in the group each player thinks is "least likely" to engage in the activity. The third is the person out of the two random people selected from the hat who would be most likely to engage in that activity (out of those two only). You may, of course, select yourself for "most" or "least" in the entire group. Keep in mind that each player is trying to match the answers of the rest of the group, so answers should depend on what each player feels everyone in the group would say. Once everyone has written their answers, each player reveals their list. Players who match all three answers with another player achieve a trifecta match and the points are tallied accordingly (see "Scoring" below.)

Player 2 then presents her activity and picks two random people from the hat, and then everyone writes down their three selections as before. The game continues until everyone has presented an interesting activity and revealed who they think are most or least likely to participate. There are endless activities you can come up with in this game.

SCORING

Players earn 5 points for every trifecta match they achieve! All three names must be in the exact same order to be a match. Players do not receive any points if even one of the three is in a different order. (For example, if Player 1 had Sandy for "most likely," Phil for "least likely," and Jennifer for "more likely than Phil" [Jennifer and Phil being the two selected from the hat], and Players 5 and 6 also had those three in that same order, all three of them would earn 10 points because each of them matched all three exactly with two other people.)

EXAMPLE

For example, for the activity "eating bugs," the two people pulled from the hat are Bob and Mary. Player 1's answer may be *John*, *Allison*, *Bob*, and Player 2 might say *John*, *Betty*, *Bob*. Both had John as "most likely" and Bob as "more likely" than Mary, BUT because they had a different person (Allison and Betty) as "least likely" in the entire group, NO MATCH!

WHAT YOU DIDN'T KNOW ABOUT BOB

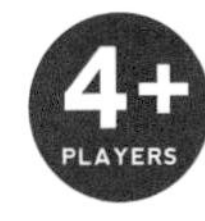

SURPRISE YOUR FRIENDS AND BE THE BEST AT FIGURING OUT THEIR SURPRISES!

PREPARATION

For each round of this game, players must come up with one surprise item about themselves in each of three categories:

1. I'm a Fan
2. I'm Not a Fan
3. On My Wish List

Here are some examples of what to place in each category:

I'm a Fan: For this category, list anything you like such as a specific movie, TV show, actor, athlete, food, place, or activity. Activities might include yoga, going to the opera, dancing, going to the beach, cycling, going to the movies, riding roller coasters, eating cereal with orange juice instead of milk, etc. (For example, you may be playing with a group of people who know many of your favorite things such as a favorite sports team or movie or vacation spot or that you love eating spaghetti and running marathons. But do they know EVERYTHING you like?! Probably not! Perhaps there's a TV show you secretly enjoy or a food you used to eat and love as a kid. Or maybe there's a silly activity you really enjoy doing but don't talk about or an actor or actress you find intriguing. You should be able to find some fun surprises in the "I'm a Fan" category.)

I'm Not a Fan: For this category, list something specific you either don't like OR have never seen, done, or tasted. In other words, it doesn't necessarily have to be something or someone you don't like. It can simply be something you have never tried, a place you have never visited, or something you have never seen such as a movie, show, event, etc. (For example, perhaps you're a world traveler and everyone knows it, but there's a city everyone thinks you probably visited that you haven't. Or maybe everyone is under the impression you couldn't possibly be afraid of anything, but panda bears absolutely freak you out.)

On My Wish List: For the wish list category, you can list a location you would love to visit, an activity you have always wanted to try, or even a specific person you have always wanted to meet. Anything really goes here, as well, but try to come up with things that very few people would know about.

Each player writes his or her "I'm a Fan" item on a small piece of paper without letting anyone see and places his or her name under the item. Each player then folds the piece of paper several times and throws it in a hat with everyone else's papers. Players do the same with their "Not a Fan" and "Wish List" items, placing those in separate piles or hats. There should now be three piles or hats with all of the "I'm a Fan" items mixed together in one separate pile, "I'm Not a Fan" items in another pile, and "Wish List" items in another.

OBJECTIVE

Players must attempt to surprise the other players by coming up with things they didn't know that player liked or disliked or always wanted to do. The biggest surprises usually score the most points.

GAME TIME

There are three rounds of this game. Place the "I'm Not a Fan" and "Wish List" piles aside for the time being. They will be used in rounds two and three. One at a time, each player picks out a random piece from the "I'm a Fan" pile and looks at it without letting anyone see what he or she picked. You may end up picking your own piece, and that's perfectly fine (though it puts you at a slight disadvantage).

Next, every player makes three columns on another piece of paper. The first column is for the list of "I'm a Fan" items. The second column should be titled *My Guesses* and is for you to fill in which player you feel is a match with each item listed. The third column titled *Correct Answers* is for you to write the correct person in the appropriate row next to each item once the answers are revealed. Then add rows to your columns to make a chart. The number of rows in the chart should be equal to the number of players. (For example, if you have six players in the game, make six rows and number them from 1 to 6 down the side of the first column.)

Player 1 then begins and reads aloud the item he selected from the hat WITHOUT revealing the person who wrote that item. Every player now has to place that item next to the number 1 on the list in the far left "I'm a Fan" column. Player 2 now reads the item she selected, and everyone places that item next to number 2 in the "I'm a Fan" column. Player 3 then reads his item, and so on. Once all of the items are read, everyone guesses which item belongs to which player and writes each player's name in column two next to the appropriate item. Obviously, you know your own, and if you didn't pick your own "I'm a Fan" item out of the hat, then you know who matches up with two of the items and you just have to figure out the rest. Once everyone is done filling out column two, the true matches are revealed for each item beginning with the first item on the list. Place the names of the players in the correct rows in column three opposite their items.

Finally, after the answers have been revealed, it's time for the Bonus Surprise Points! Every player votes for one person who he or she thinks had the most surprising "I'm a Fan" item. This is completely up to each player. You cannot vote for yourself, though. Simply look at columns one and three for the correct matches and circle the player in column three who surprised you the most with his or her "I'm a Fan" item.

Now repeat the entire process, creating three-column charts for the "I'm Not a Fan" items and then for the "On My Wish List" items. Pull the items from a hat for each round as before, and make your guesses. When total points are determined for the last category, tally up all of the points for all three categories to determine the overall winner.

WITH ONLY FOUR PLAYERS

With only four players in the game, you might decide to do all three categories at once. In other words, each player places all three of his or her items in the hat, and then everyone picks out three random pieces. Each player makes a numbered list from 1 to 12 (4 players X 3 categories). Players then take turns reading all three of their pieces. Players must guess not only the name but also the category and must place both pieces of information next to the appropriate item in column two. (For example, next to each item in column two, you would put *Jack, Fan* or *Taylor, Wish List*, or *Lisa, Not a Fan*, and so on. This provides a much greater challenge with fewer players.

SCORING

If your guess in column two matches with the correct answer in the same row in column three, you receive 1 point. In other words, players earn 1 point for every correct match. Players receive two extra points for each "Surprise" vote they get!

SAMPLE:

I'm a Fan	My Guesses	Correct Answer
Pulp Fiction	Rocky	Rocky ✓
Chocolate Chip Cookies	Lisa	Rose ✗
Peanut Butter and Tomato Sandwich	Marvin	Marvin ✓ (SURPRISE POINT)
Cheddar Cheese/Ranch Dressing	Rose	Lindsay ✗
Salsa Dancing	Lindsay	Brian ✗
Ping Pong	Brian	Lisa ✗

CALL MY BLUFF

These games offer an excellent opportunity for people in your group to be REALLY creative, to get to know each other a little bit better and perhaps make each other laugh, and to test their skills at BLUFFING! Many of the games require you to attempt to fool the other players in the room into believing you didn't say what you really said . . . and to do your best not to be fooled by everyone else!

WHO WROTE THAT?

COME UP WITH A SENTENCE NOBODY WOULD BELIEVE WAS WRITTEN BY YOU!

PREPARATION

Each player takes a separate piece of paper, writes his or her name at the top, and makes a numbered list from 1 to however many players there are in the game. (For example, if there are six players, you should have numbers 1 through 6 written vertically down your paper with enough room to write a sentence next to each number.)

Each player should tear or cut another piece of paper into equal-sized strips (one strip per player in the game) and place them in the middle for all players to use. This should give you enough paper strips to complete one round per player.

OBJECTIVE

In each round, players must come up with a sentence that the other players in the game would think was written by someone else . . . and then figure out who wrote all of the other sentences!

GAME TIME

Players take turns coming up with an object or person to write about. It can be anything: *a bar of soap, a pumpkin, an iguana, earwax, Cousin Gretchen*, etc. The player who chooses the subject announces it to the group. Each player must then come up with a sentence of between five and ten words about that chosen subject and write it on one of the strips of paper. The sentence doesn't have to be true or make any sense whatsoever!

> **IMPORTANT:** Make sure your sentence is completely legible! It is advised to not write in cursive. Perhaps even write in block letters so not only is there no question anyone will be able to read it but the person reading it won't be able to tell who wrote it.

Each player must then fold his paper several times and place it in a hat or bowl mixed in with all of the other players' sentences. Each player then randomly picks out a sentence to read. (You may even end up picking your own.)

Player 1 goes first and reads the sentence he picked out without making any gesture as to who he thinks wrote the sentence. That is sentence number 1, and everyone writes it next to number 1 on their paper. Player 2 reads the next sentence, which is sentence number 2, and everyone writes it next to number 2 on their paper. Play continues as the remaining players read the sentence they picked out until all sentences are read and written down.

> **IMPORTANT:** When you are reading a sentence, you don't want to give away who you think wrote it if, for instance, you recognize the handwriting or you just know someone really well. You want to be the only one to guess correctly and get the points. (More on that under "Scoring.")

Each player must now write down the name of the person they think wrote each sentence next to the sentence on the page. Circle your own name so the person scoring your answers knows not to give you credit for that sentence. Once everyone is done placing an author next to each sentence, players pass their score sheets to the left. That player will score your sheet for you.

Once the sheets have been passed, the author of each sentence is revealed one at a time and points are tallied.

Player 2 now comes up with a subject to write about to play a second round.

SCORING

Players earn 10 points for every answer they match with the right player (your own sentence doesn't count, of course) and 5 points for every player who didn't guess which sentence was theirs. The player with the most points after each round wins, or keep track of the scores for each round for a grand total at the end.

EXAMPLE

Let's say there are seven players in the game. Player 1 selects *Pumpkin* as his topic, so each player (including Player 1) writes a sentence about a pumpkin and places it in the hat. All players then choose a sentence from the hat, and the game begins.

After all the guesses have been written down and the sheets passed to the left, it is time to find out who wrote each sentence. Player 1 goes first and reads the sentence he picked out of the hat: "My pumpkin ate my dog." Player 2 reveals that she is the author. Points are awarded to players who got it right. If three players (other than Player 2) guessed correctly, those three players each earn 10 points and Player

2 earns 15 points (5 X 3) for the three other players who were fooled.

Player 2 then reads the next sentence, and Player 5 reveals that he is the author. Nobody guessed that he was the author, so Player 5 gets 30 points (5 X 6).

SAMPLE:

1) My pumpkin ate my dog.

2) Pumpkin is best when served on a stick.

3) My pumpkin looks like uncle Jack.

4) Never take pumpkin on a road trip.

5) I always said Levon is half man, half pumpkin.

6) Patty Pumpkin played with Peter.

7) Clearly Phil ate way too much pumpkin last night.

WHO DIDN'T WRITE THAT?

SUBSTITUTE YOUR SENTENCE FOR SOMEONE ELSE'S AND SEE HOW MANY YOU CAN FOOL!

PREPARATION

Each player takes a separate piece of paper, writes his or her name at the top, and makes a numbered list from 1 to however many players there are in the game. (For example, if there are six players, you should have numbers 1 through 6 written vertically down your paper with enough room to write a sentence next to each number.)

Each player should tear or cut another piece of paper into equal-size strips (one strip per player in the game) and place them in the middle for all players to use. This should give you enough paper strips to complete one round per player.

OBJECTIVE

Players try to write something that nobody would think they wrote. The player who comes up with the subject substitutes his or her own sentence for one of the other player's sentences, and everyone has to figure out which sentence was substituted.

GAME TIME

Players, starting with Player 1, take turns coming up with an object or person to write about. Player 1 comes up with a subject. Everyone writes a sentence (five to ten words) on the subject, labeled with their name, and hands it to Player 1. Player 1 then substitutes his own sentence for one of the other players', removing that sentence from the pile. He then writes the name of the person he substituted his sentence for on the substituted sentence paper.

> **NOTE:** The player coming up with the subject and reading the sentences should try to write a sentence which most people would believe was definitely written by the person he is choosing for the substitution.

Player 1 reads the adjusted set of sentences aloud in a random order, along with the name of the player who wrote each sentence (replacing his own name with that of the player whose sentence he replaced).

> **NOTE:** Player 1 doesn't associate his name with any sentence because he is pretending one of the other players wrote his sentence. Therefore, if there are seven total players in the game, Player 1 will read only six sentences, each one associated with another one of the other six players in the game.

Once Player 1 is done reading all the sentences, the other players must figure out which of the sentences was substituted. Everyone writes down the name of the person whose sentence they feel was substituted, and when pens are down, the guesses are revealed.

> **IMPORTANT:** Obviously, if Player 1 substituted his sentence for Player 2's, Player 2 will know and write down her own name, but she won't earn any points for that. Instead, the substituted player will get credit for all the people who were fooled by Player 1's substitution. Therefore, the substituted player must not give away that her sentence was substituted until after the guesses are made!

SCORING

The player who comes up with the subject and is responsible for substituting a sentence earns 5 points for every player who is fooled. The player whose sentence was substituted also earns 5 points for every player who guessed wrong.

Finally, each player who did not have his or her sentence substituted has the opportunity to earn 5 points for guessing the correct answer and another 5 points for every player who chose his or her sentence as the one that was substituted.

EXAMPLE

Let's say, in a game with five players, Player 1 substituted his sentence for Player 2's. All the players write down their guesses and then reveal them. One player guessed correctly that the sentence read did NOT belong to Player 2. Two players think (incorrectly) that Player 3's sentence was substituted. Player 1 does not guess, and Player 2 already knows the answer, so scoring begins. Player 1 and Player 2 both earn 10 points because they fooled two players. The player who guessed correctly earns 5 points. Player 3 earns 10 points because his sentence fooled two other players.

QUESTIONS AND ANSWERS

CAN YOU COME UP WITH A CREATIVE QUESTION THAT WILL MATCH THE ANSWER?

PREPARATION

All players must come up with a question and answer about someone in the game. Each player writes the question on one piece of paper and the answer on another piece. Players should also set aside extra paper for writing guesses.

> **TIP:** The question and answer can be silly, funny, true, or false—anything goes! But be sure to come up with a question no one would guess that you would ask. (Even better if you can make it seem like the type of question someone else in the game would ask.)

OBJECTIVE

Players try to come up with creative questions which match with the answer provided for maximum points.

GAME TIME

Player 1 begins by sharing the answer—and ONLY the answer—to his question with the group. He keeps the question to himself for the time being. The rest of the players must now come up with a question that can be answered by Player 1's answer.

> **TIP:** Try to come up with a question everyone would believe was written by Player 1. You are essentially trying to fool others into believing your question was created by the person who came up with the original question and answer. Also be sure that your question is as creative as possible.

Players hand their corresponding questions to Player 1 without letting anyone else see them.

> **IMPORTANT:** Make sure your question is completely legible! If not, Player 1 will hand it back to you to write again.

Once Player 1 receives all of the questions from the other players, he mixes his original question in with theirs and then reads them all in random order without revealing who wrote each question.

Now, all the other players in the game write down two questions. The first is the one they believe is the original question from Player 1. The second is the one they each think is the most creative, interesting, or humorous. This "creativity vote" is completely arbitrary; there are no wrong answers. However, you may not give your own question your creativity vote!

Player 1 writes down only his creativity vote since he obviously knows the original. Once the original question is revealed, Player 1 tallies the scores (see "Scoring").

Play continues as players take turns sharing their answers (one per round) and everyone comes up with questions to match each new answer.

SCORING

In each round, the player who comes up with the original question and answer earns 5 points for every player who doesn't guess which one was his or her original question and 5 points for every player who also gives his or her original question the creativity vote.

The other players earn 5 points for guessing the original question correctly and 5 points for every creativity vote their question earned.

> **IMPORTANT:** If a player comes up with the question that actually matches the original, that player gets the same points in that round as the player who came up with that original question. The player leading the round will not reveal it until the end, though, and doesn't read that question twice. Everyone will simply know that someone matched the original when they see that one question is missing.

EXAMPLE

For instance, in a game of four players, Player 1 may present the answer "Every Sunday." The other players write down questions that could match, like *When does Jack usually have a lot of gas?* or *When does Richard shave his chest?* or *When do Conner and Bob give each other pedicures?* Player 1's original question was actually *When does Bob take a three-hour nap?* If only one of the other three players correctly identified the original question, Player 1 earns 10 points (2 X 5) and the player who guessed correctly earns 5 points. If three players voted for Player 3's question (*When does Rich-*

ard shave his chest?) as the most creative, Player 3 earns 15 points.

TIP: In this game, it is easier and more fun when players provide simple answers such as "Yes," "No," "True," "False," "Never in a million years," "When pigs fly," or any number- or time frame-based answer, as with the above example. Answers like that open the door for many possible questions and a lot of creativity . . . and that is where the game becomes most entertaining! When the answer is very specific, it can still be fun, of course, but the question options are more limited and multiple people might provide the same or similar questions.

THREE OF A KIND

INDEX CARDS RECOMMENDED

BE THE ONLY ONE TO FIND THE THREE ITEMS THAT GO TOGETHER!

PREPARATION

To start, everyone needs to write down three related words or items; e.g., rye, wheat, and white (breads); rabbit, fish, and bird (pets); *scream, dream,* and *steam* (words that rhyme); Goofy, Pluto, and Donald Duck (Disney characters); or Deniro, Redford, and Pattinson (all Roberts). Players write these three-of-a-kind words or items on three separate index cards without letting the other players see what they have written.

> **NOTE:** Be creative, but keep in mind that you don't want to make your three too easy or too difficult for people to figure out.

As the other players are writing down three items for the first round, the first player to finish must also create "Bluff Cards." A Bluff Card is an index card with the word *Bluff* written on it, and these same cards can be used for all subsequent rounds. To determine the number of Bluff Cards needed, take the total number of players in the game and subtract 3. (For example, if you have seven players in the game, you will need four Bluff Cards.) Make sure you write lightly on the index cards with pens or pencils so the words won't show through on the other side.

OBJECTIVE

In this game, players need to use their best bluffing skills! Players try to fool everyone else into thinking they drew a different card than the one they actually drew while trying to guess the real three-of-a-kind match. The fewer players who guess the real three of a kind correctly, the more points those players receive.

GAME TIME

Player 1 holds on to one of his three index cards and mixes the other two with all of the Bluff Cards facedown so no one can see them. Then he asks each player, starting with the player to his left, to randomly draw a card without revealing to anyone which card he or she picked. Once a player sees what is written on the chosen card, he or she hides it until later.

Players who draw a Bluff Card must try to make people believe they picked one of Player 1's three-of-a-kind set. Players who drew one of the three-of-a-kind cards must say the word on the card when it is their turn; the catch is that these players want to make the rest of the players think they are bluffing.

Player 1 goes first and says the word on the card he held back for himself. Player 2 then says a related word. If Player 2 drew one of Player 1's three-of-a-kind cards, she must say that word; if she drew a bluff card, she must try to convince the other players that whatever word she makes up is the real match to Player 1's word.

IMPORTANT: If a person with a Bluff Card actually says one of the two real words in the three-of-a-kind set before the person who actually has the word gets to say it, the roles reverse, and the person who actually has the word must now bluff and come up with something else which will make people choose his or her new word as part of the three-of-a-kind group.

Players who happen to select one of the three-of-a-kind cards at the beginning have a major advantage because they already know two of the words; they only need to guess the third.

After every player in the game has had the chance to bluff or say the word on his card, each player must write down his or her three-of-a-kind guess. Once all of the guesses are written down, it's pens down! Players cannot change their guesses during the reveal.

Once the scores are tallied, Player 2 begins a new round with her three-of-a-kind set, and play continues until all players have had the chance to lead a round.

SCORING

For the players who guessed correctly, the amount of points they each receive is equivalent to ten times the number of people who got it wrong! (For example, with six players in the game, not including Player 1, if four got it wrong and two got it right, those two players who got it right would each earn 40 points.) The players who got it wrong don't earn any points.

The player who created the three-of-a-kind set earns 50 points if (1) at least one person gets it right AND (2) no more than half of the guessers get it right. If more than half of the players get it right, Player 1 gets no points at all. In addition—and this is important—if either nobody or everybody guesses correctly, Player 1 loses 20 points and every other player in the game earns 20 points.

This point system is put in place to make sure everyone tries their hardest to fool everyone else and to encourage players to make their three-of-a-kind set challenging, but not too challenging.

EXAMPLE

Using one of the examples above (pets: rabbit, fish, and bird), let's say Player 1 kept *fish* for himself and mixed *rabbit* and *bird* in with the Bluff Cards. Player 1 starts by simply saying "Fish." Now Player 2 has to say a word. Player 2 drew a Bluff Card; now she must say something that she believes goes with *fish* so everyone thinks her word is part of the three-of-a-kind set. She decides to say "Shark." Now it's Player 3's turn. If Player 3 drew the *rabbit* card, he must say "Rabbit," but he can hesitate to make people think he has a Bluff Card.

Let's say Player 5 drew the *bird* card, but before he has the chance to use it, Player 4 bluffs and says "Bird." Player 5, who actually had *bird*, must now think of something else to make everyone think he has one of the three-of-a-kind cards. Additionally, Player 5 now knows that Player 4 drew one of the Bluff Cards, but Player 4 doesn't necessarily know that she came up with one of the real three-of-a-kind items when she was bluffing. This makes for an interesting set of circumstances, and the bluffs—and the stakes—build.

For scoring, let's say there are seven players in the above example with pets. After every player takes his or her turn, everyone writes down their guesses (except Player 1, of course) as to what they think are the real three of a kind. If two of the six players guessing get it right, those two players earn 40 points (10 times the four players who guessed incorrectly). The four who were wrong do not earn any points. Player 1 earns 50 points because at least one person got it right and no more than half got it right. However, if four of the six players guessing got it right, then those four players would each earn 20 points (10 times the two players who guessed incorrectly) and Player 1 would not earn any points since more than half of the players guessing got it right. Essentially, the three of a kind was too easy. Keep in mind though, if everyone or nobody guesses correctly, Player 1 loses 20 points and everyone else gets 20.

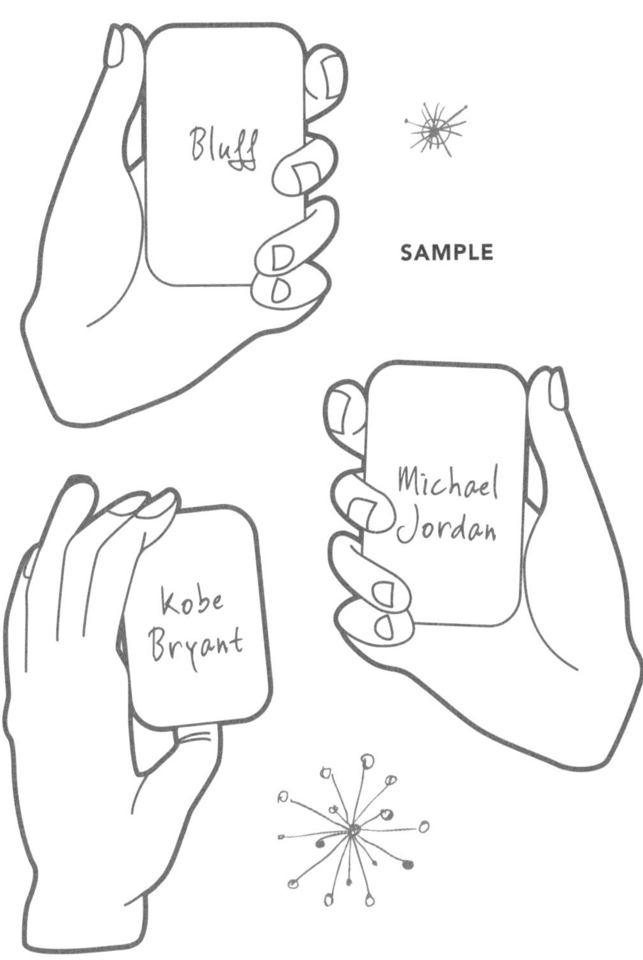

LIAR, LIAR, PANTS ON FIRE

TEST YOUR ACTING SKILLS UNDER EXTREME PRESSURE!

PREPARATION

For each round of this game, players must come up with something interesting that has happened in their lives that most people in the group (if not all) don't know about; the ideal scenario in this game is for nobody to know about it.

> **NOTE:** For some groups, including family members, this may be a difficult task. Still, you should be able to think of something you did—some big or small event you witnessed or perhaps someone you met (maybe even a celebrity)—that you never told anyone in your group about.

Each player writes this experience or event down in as few words as possible on a piece of paper with his or her name written underneath. Again, use very few words. For example, short phrases like *Met Bill Murray* or *Witnessed a car crash* or *Saw someone vomit on the subway* or *Got a rash from eating strawberries* or *Saw a streaker at a baseball game* work well.

You must make sure your writing is completely legible! If not, your item will be thrown out by the person who tries to read it.

Once every player has an event written down with their name, all players crumple their papers into a ball and place them in a hat with everyone else's papers. Now each player makes a numbered list (from 1 to the total number of players in the game) on a separate piece of paper, leaving enough room next to each number to write down the event.

OBJECTIVE

Players try to fool other players into believing that a completely fabricated story actually happened (or that a true story is just a well-conceived lie).

GAME TIME

One at a time, players pick out a crumpled piece of paper, and everyone opens their paper without letting anyone see what they have. Player 1 goes first and announces the event he picked, but he does not reveal the player who wrote it. Everyone writes the event down next to the number 1 on his piece of paper.

Every player, beginning with Player 2, must try to make everyone else believe that the event Player 1 announced was his or hers! Every player tries to come up with a convincing story to persuade the group, then yields the floor to the next player, and so on until it gets back to Player 1, who will also take a turn convincing everyone that he was the one who actually had the experience he read aloud. Of course, one person in the group will actually be telling the truth, and that player MUST tell the truth, but he or she really wants everyone to believe he or she is making it up like everyone else in the game.

Each player can decide how detailed his or her story will be, but every story must include three basic elements:

1. Where it happened
2. When it happened
3. Who you were with when it happened

Once every player has told his or her story about the event, all players write down who they think really submitted that event next to the event on their numbered page. (You can certainly change your mind at the end of the game, but for now, you are making a note about who you think told the truth about that specific event.)

NOTE: The true storyteller writes his or her own name next to the story, and the person who picked it out of the hat also writes that storyteller's name down. Although both of these players know the answer, you never want to give away to anyone that you know the truth, so you should pretend to be thinking about your guess like everyone else. There's also the possibility that you will pick your own story out of the hat. In that case, you are the ONLY player who really knows the truth when the stories are being told.

The next round begins as Player 2 announces the event she drew from the hat, and everyone (beginning with Player 3) pretends that this event happened to him or her as well. Players must do their best to convince everyone in the game that every single story they are telling is true—even though ultimately only one story from each player is factual. Go around the room telling stories for every event in the hat. Each time a player tells a story about an event, the other players should make notes as to who they believe and who they don't believe. After every player tells his or her story about the last event, all players come up with their final list of matches. Which event actually happened to each player? Once every player has his or her final answers clearly written next to each event on the numbered piece of paper, players reveal which story they told was actually true and the points are calculated (see "Scoring").

SCORING

Players receive 10 points for every story they match with the correct person. You don't get credit for your own story, but you get an easy 10 points if you picked a story out of the hat that wasn't yours. Players also receive 10 points for every player who doesn't guess their true story. (In other words, players earn points for every player they fool!)

EXAMPLE

For example, let's say the event Player 1 picked out was "Met Bill Murray." Player 2 must now pretend that it happened to her, even if it didn't. When Player 2 is done, Player 3 will do the same for the Bill Murray story. But in keeping with the three rules above, each player's response length will vary. Player 2 might say something like "I met Bill Murray four years ago in San Francisco with my friend Jack" and stop there. Player 3 might elaborate a bit more and say, "We were eating breakfast, and Bill came up to us and asked us how we liked our pancakes." Either way, it is your job to make people think it is actually your story if it isn't.

For scoring, let's say there are seven players in the example game above. If four people guessed who REALLY met Bill Murray, those four would each earn 10 points. The person who actually met Bill Murray would receive 20 points (10 times the two players who guessed that it was someone else).

IMPORTANT: For the person who REALLY met Bill Murray (or whatever the event is), that person must tell the truth about the story when it is his or her turn, but that player can still add some bluffing elements to his or her storytelling as long as everything he or she is saying is true. For example, that player might go on and on about the story, including true facts which seem ridiculous just to make people think he or she is lying. Sometimes, the person with the true story will hesitate on the facts just to make people believe he or she is putting too much thought into a fake story.

STORYTELLERS

HAVING TOO MUCH FUN MAKING UP STORIES!

PREPARATION

Each player must come up with two fun made-up events he or she wants other players to talk about as if they really happened. (For example, an event such as "I was attacked by a pack of angry squirrels in the Grand Canyon but was luckily rescued by a supermodel in a golf cart." Or "I was on a long flight to Hong Kong and the guy next to me just kept slapping me in the face every 30 minutes for no reason." Or "I was with the president the other day and a talking kangaroo came over and peed on our breakfast." You get the picture.)

Every player writes each of the two events legibly on separate pieces of paper and then crumples each piece in a ball and places it in a hat or on a table mixed up with all of the others.

OBJECTIVE

Players must each talk about three strange events as if they really happened in their lives, using two events they pick from the hat and adding one of their own without giving away which event is the one they added. Guessers must figure out which two of the three events were picked from the pile and which one was added.

GAME TIME

Player 1 goes first and picks two random events from the hat without showing anyone what he picked. If he picks one of his own, he must put that one back, mix it back up in the hat, and pick another. Then Player 2 picks two random events from the hat. Again, if any event she picks is her own submission, she must put it back and pick again. Every player in the game follows the same process until the last player. The last player picks out the final two events. If either one of them belongs to him or her, that player must toss the event away and ask each player in the game to come up with another event, crumple it up, and throw it in the pile. The last player will then pick again. This ensures that nobody tells a story which incorporates an event he or she submitted at the beginning for someone else to tell.

In this game, a complete story for each player consists of three events. So before Player 1 begins the storytelling, players take two minutes to decide what made-up event they wish to add to their story. The object is to make people believe this event was provided by someone else in the game. Players write down their third event on one of the pieces of paper so they are ready to go with all three when it is their turn.

When Player 1 begins telling his story about three random events that happened in his life, he can begin with any of the three events and tell them in any order. Either way, it is fun when everyone starts their storytelling by saying something like "Did I ever tell you guys about the time I . . ." Then, after talking about the first event, players can say, "Oh, and then there was that time I . . ." and continue on with the second event and so on.

Players can also ad lib as much as they want to with each of the three events. That's another element that makes the storytelling so much fun.

TIP: Try to keep the time allotted for each player's stories to less than 5 minutes. You can even tell everyone about all three events in less than 1 minute, if you'd like, just giving the basic details.

After Player 1 is done telling his complete story about all three memorable events in his life, he then asks the rest of the players, "Which of these events did I add myself?" To make it clear, Player 1 numbers each of the stories that he told. The rest of the players must decide which story Player 1 added himself. Players write down their guesses, and on the count of three, the guesses are all revealed at once.

Every player goes around the room telling fun stories while also trying to disguise his added event.

EXAMPLE

Using the above sample events, let's say Player 1 picked out the following two events from the hat: (1) *I was attacked by a pack of angry squirrels in the Grand Canyon but was luckily rescued by a supermodel in a golf cart.* and (2) *I was on a long flight to Hong Kong and the guy next to me just kept slapping me in the face every 30 minutes for no reason.* Player 1 will now have to add another event to talk about. For example, he may add "My grandmother was a champion yogurt wrestler and always made the family wrestle in different flavored yogurts every Friday night."

SCORING

For every story, players each earn 5 points if they guess correctly. The storyteller earns 3 points for every player who gets it wrong. (Every time one of YOUR submitted events is one of the events in the story of another player, you have a 50/50 chance of guessing correctly. If you were lucky enough to have one player pick out both of your events, you will win easy points for that player's story.)

HOW WELL CAN YOU DISGUISE YOUR ARTISTIC TALENTS?

PREPARATION

Players take turns coming up with an interesting object for the group to draw (e.g., a haunted house, an upside-down car, a bird with gigantic eyes, a gorilla on roller skates, etc.). The object certainly doesn't have to be simple; it can be fun, silly, and even complicated.

> **IMPORTANT:** Players should all use the exact same color and type of writing instruments (e.g., all pencils or all blue pens). And do not let anyone see what you are drawing!

OBJECTIVE

Players must attempt to disguise their own drawing style and determine who drew all of the other pictures.

GAME TIME

Starting with Player 1's object, every player must draw that same object. Allow up to two minutes for drawing time.

NOTE: You must make some real attempt at drawing a picture. You can't just draw a few lines, and no stick figures are allowed. Also, if your drawing skills are quite good or you have a specific style and everyone knows it, you may want to come up with a series of new drawing styles for this game!

When everyone is finished drawing, players place their completed pictures facedown at the center of the table. Player 1 mixes the pictures up and then turns them over and numbers them, writing a number on the top of each picture clearly enough for everyone to see. Players must now determine who drew each picture. Players make their lists, which might look something like this:

Picture 1: John
Picture 2: Mary
Picture 3: Katherine, etc.

Play continues as players reveal their drawings, tally points, and then move on to the next player's object.

SCORING

Players earn 1 point for every player they fool and 1 point for every picture they match correctly.

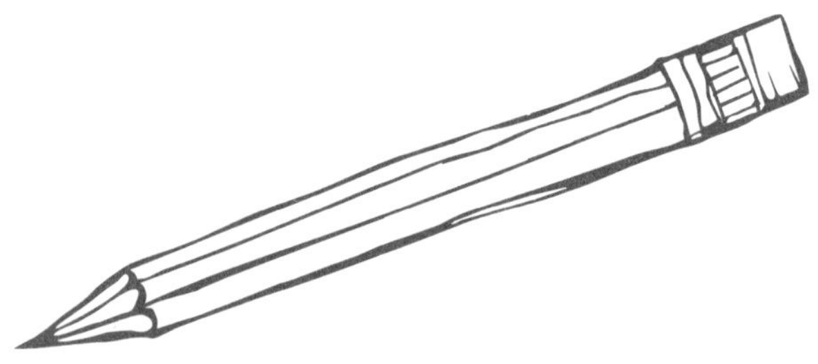

LEFT AND RIGHT

WHO REALLY SAID THAT?

PREPARATION

Players sit or stand in a circle.

OBJECTIVE

One player in each round makes the ultimate decision on which two-word phrase to use and tries to fool others in the game with help from the players on his or her left and right. Guessers do their best to figure it out!

GAME TIME

Player 1 asks the player to his left and the player to his right, one at a time, to whisper a two-word phrase in his ear. (Any two words will do, and they don't have to actually go together or make any sense.)

Player 1 then decides if he is going to use one of their phrases or come up with one of his own.

> **NOTE:** When you are sitting to the left or right of the player leading the round (Player 1 for the first round) and are being asked to come up with a two-word phrase, the key is to come up with two words nobody

would ever think you said. At the same time, if Player 1 decides not to use either phrase provided to him from his left or right, he must come up with a new one that other players will believe is something the player to the left or right might say.

Once Player 1 makes the decision, he says the two-word phrase out loud to the rest of the players. The other players must now decide who came up with that phrase. Was it Player 1 or one of the players to his left or right? Everyone reveals their answer at once by pointing to the player they select, and all players tally their points. Play continues as Player 2 gets phrases from the players to her left and right, and so on.

SCORING

Players earn points if they are able to fool the other players. The player who leads the round and the players to his or her left and right each get 1 point for every player who is fooled. If a player guesses correctly, he or she earns 2 points.

JIMMY PLAYED WITH BETTY'S NOSTRILS (JPWBN)

GET CREATIVE WITH ACRONYMS!

PREPARATION

Player 1 begins and comes up with any letter and announces it. Player 2 comes up with a second letter. Player 3 comes up with another, and so on until there are five letters. All players write the letters down at the top of a piece of paper in the order they were provided. Players also number a separate sheet of paper vertically from 1 to the total number of players in the game.

OBJECTIVE

Each player must come up with the most creative sentence/phrase from five randomly selected letters to earn the most votes and, thus, the most points.

GAME TIME

Each player in the game must now come up with a creative five-word sentence using those starting letters in the order they were given.

> **IMPORTANT:** The sentences don't need to make sense, but be sure to write clearly and legibly. Someone will need to be able to read your sentence, and you don't want people passing around your sentence for clarification!

When everyone is finished, all players crumple their sentence into a ball and place it in the middle of the table, and Player 1 mixes them up. Now each player randomly picks one up to read.

Player 1 writes the number 1 on the first sentence, announces, "Here is sentence number 1," and reads it aloud without revealing who he thinks wrote the sentence. (The authors will not be revealed until the very end.) After Player 1 reads the first sentence, each player (including Player 1) writes the sentence down next to number 1 on his or her paper. Player 2 then places the number 2 on the sentence she has, announces that it is sentence number 2, and reads it aloud for everyone to write down next to number 2. Continue on like this until all sentences have been read. Every player then looks at them all again and votes for the top two most creative, interesting, or funny sentences. (If there are more than eight players in the game, everyone should vote for the top three sentences.)

One at a time, each player reveals which two sentences he or she wants to vote for, and Player 1 (or the player leading the round) tallies points. After the authors reveal themselves and points are awarded, the next round begins. For the next round, Player 2 selects the first letter, Player 3 selects the next, and so on.

NOTE: You cannot vote for your own sentence!

SCORING

The person with the sentence that receives the most votes earns 20 points, second place earns 10, and third earns 5. If there is a tie for first, each of those players get 20 points. If there is a tie for second, each of those players get 10 points, and so on.

EXAMPLE

Let's say the letters for this round, in order of selection from Player 1 to Player 5, are JPWBN. For these letters, one might say "Jimmy played with Betty's nostrils" or "Joanne painted Wally's blue newt" or "Joe Pesci wanted bigger napkins." Be as creative as possible.

SAMPLE:

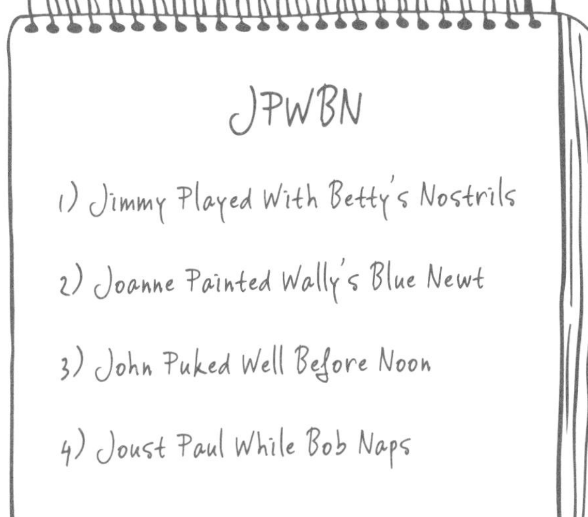

JPWBN
1) Jimmy Played With Betty's Nostrils
2) Joanne Painted Wally's Blue Newt
3) John Puked Well Before Noon
4) Joust Paul While Bob Naps

THAT'S MY PLAN, AND I'M STICKING TO IT!

These games all require some sort of strategy that will enable you to have the best chance to win. As always, you don't have to keep score to have fun, but for many of the games, you'll find that a scoring system such as the one presented is important for the optimal experience.

RISK IT OR NOT!

TAKE A RISK WITH A FEW BIG WORDS, OR BE CONSERVATIVE WITH MANY SMALL WORDS.

PREPARATION

Every player draws twenty-five dashes in one long line.

OBJECTIVE

The objective is to spell words over the twenty-five dashes using the letters provided by all of the players until all twenty-five dashes are used. The longer each word is in each player's string, the more points he or she gets.

GAME TIME

Starting with Player 1 and going clockwise around the table, each player says one random letter, and everyone must put that letter on one of the twenty-five dashes. Once placed in a slot, that letter cannot be moved, so strategize before writing a letter down. Continue going around the circle saying letters until all twenty-five slots are filled. Letters can be repeated.

TIP: The longer the word, the bigger the risk. You may not get the letters you want for that word and you'll be stuck with few words and a low-scoring board. On the other hand, if you decide to risk it all and your big words pan out, your score will be high. But be warned: the more players in the game, the less control you have over the letters selected and the more difficult it will be to score long words.

IMPORTANT: The same letter CANNOT be used for more than one word! (For example, you can't use the *P* in *STOP* as the first letter in a new word that begins with *P*. But see below for the "Word Nerd" version.)

In each round, a different player should go first. To give every player a chance to go first, the number of rounds played should be equal to the number of players in the game.

SCORING

The number of letters in a word multiplied by itself is the amount of points you get for that word.

WORD NERD BONUS SCORING

In this version, players can strategize to overlap words in order to get the most points out of their letters. In addition, words within words count as well. Scoring follows the same principles as regular play—the number of letters in a word squared. (For example, the word *friend* would still be worth 36 points (6 X 6), but clever players would also see the word *end* in *friend* and add an additional 9 points (3 X 3).

EXAMPLE (REGULAR SCORING)

Once all twenty-five letters are chosen, a final game board for Player 1 might look like this:

F R I E N D A J P L O W L E K C R A M P E D S S A

Player 1 earns 36 points for FRIEND (6 X 6), 16 points for PLOW (4 X 4), and 49 points for CRAMPED (7 X 7) for a total of 101 points. Player 2's game board in the same round (using the same letters, of course) might look like this:

P A M P E R D R J A W A K E N C D F L O S S E I L

She earns 36 points for PAMPER (6 X 6), 36 points for AWAKEN (6 X 6), and 25 points for FLOSS (5 X 5) for a total of 97 points.

GOTCHA!

FIGURE OUT WHAT THEY ARE GOING TO SPELL AND SPOIL THEIR FUN!

PREPARATION

Write all the letters of the alphabet on separate pieces of paper. Mix them up and place them facedown on a table or in a hat where nobody can see them. (You may want to consider leaving out *Q*, *X*, and *Z*.)

OBJECTIVE

Players take turns pairing up to try and spell words together without either player knowing in advance what word they are going to spell.

GAME TIME

Player 1 picks a letter out of the hat. Players 1 and 2 now take turns spelling a word, one letter at a time, beginning with the letter Player 1 picked out of the hat. (No names or plurals allowed!) Player 2 now says one random letter. Player 1 says a random letter, and Player 2 says a fourth letter. After four letters, the game is put on pause and the rest of the players in the game must guess what word Players 1 and 2 are going to spell. Each player writes his or her guess on a piece of paper (without sharing the guess with anyone) and places the guess facedown in the center of the table with his or her name on it.

Then Players 1 and 2 continue spelling their word, all the time never communicating with each other. Players 1 and 2 should never talk other than to exchange letters. Once Player 1 or Player 2 thinks they are done spelling the word, that player says "Stop." Either player can say "Stop" at any time. At that point, all players turn over their guesses to see if anyone was correct, and points are awarded.

Play continues when Player 3 draws a new first letter and Players 3 and 4 take a turn trying to spell a new word. Change up the pairings on each round.

SCORING

If at least one player guessed the word correctly, that player and anyone else who guessed the word each earn 50 points and Players 1 and 2 lose 50 points each! The other players in the game get no points.

However, if nobody guessed the word, Players 1 and 2 multiply the number of letters in their word by 10, and that is how many points they each earn. Nobody else loses or earns any points.

> **IMPORTANT:** If the two players misspell a word, they each lose 10 times the amount of letters in the word they created, and everyone else in the game earns 25 points.
>
> In addition, if Player 1 or Player 2 thinks at any time while spelling that they are in danger of not spelling a word at all or spelling one incorrectly, the player should say "Stop!" immediately. In this case, multiply the number of letters already used in the incomplete word by 10, and that is how many points Players 1 and 2 each

lose in that round. Again, everyone else in the game earns 25 points each.

EXAMPLE

If the letter picked out of the hat by Player 1 is R and the next three random letters chosen brought the word to REPU, then some possible guesses could include *republic, reputable, repugnant, reputation*, etc. (Remember, plurals of words are not allowed.)

If the word ended up being *reputation* and nobody guessed it, the total points for Players 1 and 2 would be 100 (10 X 10). However, if one person got it right, that person would earn 50 points, and Players 1 and 2 would each lose 50 points!

SPELLING BEE

A MADE-UP, FUN WORD-SPELLING CONTEST!

PREPARATION

Players take turns coming up with a made-up word, such as "scratchamytoesis" or "flabborizer" or "juicetastible."

OBJECTIVE

Players make up a word and try to trick the other players into spelling it incorrectly.

GAME TIME

Player 1 begins by writing down his word without letting anyone see and then pronounces it aloud to the group. He places the correct spelling facedown on the table with his name on it.

Each player then writes down what he or she thinks is the correct spelling of that word and puts his or her pen down when ready. One by one, each player reveals his or her guess.

TIP: Players may ask for the part of speech or to hear the word in a sentence, and the player who provided the word must oblige.

SCORING

Each player who spells the word correctly earns 20 points. Player 1 (or whoever came up with the word for the round) earns 10 points for each player who gets it wrong with one important exception: if nobody spells the word correctly, Player 1 loses 50 points for that round and every other player earns 10 points.

> **TIP:** Make your word hard, but not too hard! In this game, you want only one person to get it right to earn the maximum amount of points for your word.

GET EVERYONE TO GUESS YOUR LIST OF FAMOUS PEOPLE IN AS FEW CLUES AS POSSIBLE.

PREPARATION

Each player makes a list of twenty famous people and writes each of them on individual, small pieces of paper with his or her own name underneath each one. These are the game pieces, which are all mixed up in a hat or other object to prevent anyone from seeing them.

OBJECTIVE

Players must try to get all of the other players in the game to guess their "famous person" picks in as few clues as possible—preferably just one!

GAME TIME

Player 1 goes first and picks a number of pieces out of the hat without looking or letting anyone else see who he picked. The number of pieces chosen is equivalent to the number of players in the game, not including the player who draws the pieces.

Player 1 must now try and get all of the other players in the game to guess one of the famous people he picked using only one-word clues and a maximum of three clues per name. It is up to Player 1 to determine which player will guess each famous person from the names he drew.

Players can assign the famous people they drew to whichever players they choose with one exception: players may not ask a player to guess one of the famous people he or she submitted to the pile. (That is why everyone puts their names underneath each famous person they submit.)

TIP: The player giving the clues should determine which player is most likely to guess each famous person based on his or her interests.

Player 1 selects the player he wants to have guess his first famous person and gives the first clue. Players can use one-word clues ONLY, and no clue can be any part of the person's name. (For example, if you want someone to guess "Sylvester Stallone," your first clue could be "Rocky." If you want someone to say "Marlon Brando," your first clue could be "Godfather.")

Each player in the game MUST have the chance to attempt to guess one of the selections. Players may not skip anyone or use a player twice. Each player in the game has no more than 30 seconds after each clue. Once Player 1 has either succeeded or failed to elicit correct guesses from each of the other players, play continues with Player 2, who draws the same number of names from the hat and assigns them to the other players to guess.

NOTE: Once a game piece is used, it must be tossed away. Also, if a famous person is selected from the hat who has already been used in the game (for example, if more than one person submitted "Will Ferrell"), toss it away and pick again. There should be enough submissions to negate the loss of a few duplicates.

SCORING

If the player who Player 1 selected to guess a name guesses correctly with just one clue, both players earn 3 points. If the player guesses in two clues, both players earn 2 points. In three clues, both players earn 1 point each. If a player doesn't guess correctly in three clues, neither player (the guesser or the clue giver) gets any points and Player 1 moves on to the next player with a new name. For example, if there are five total players in the game, you can earn a maximum of 12 points (3 X 4 [the other four players]) each time it is your turn to pick the game pieces and give clues.

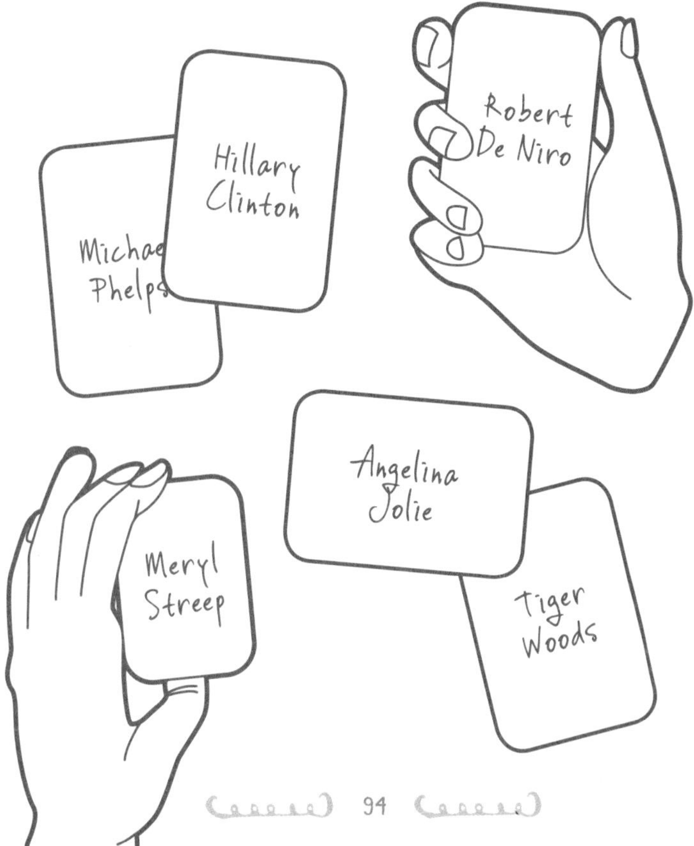

CLUES!

INDEX CARDS RECOMMENDED

COME UP WITH THE RIGHT CLUES FOR SPECIFIC MOVIES, MUSIC GROUPS, AND TV SHOWS!

PREPARATION

Player 1 goes first, so all of the other players must come up with a TV show, movie, or music group or performer they feel Player 1 would know well.

> **NOTE:** You don't have to include all three categories (movies, TV shows, and music groups or performers) in your game. You can simply pick one category for each round, and then everyone has to come up with an item from that specific category. Other categories work for this game as well, such as books, Broadway shows or musicals, or even geography for a group of world travelers.

Each player writes the name of the show, movie, and/or group on an index card in large, legible writing and holds it out in front of him or her for everyone to see. Players keep their cards out in front of them during the entire round so everyone has a full view of all the selections while Player 1 is giving the clues.

> **IMPORTANT:** If two people come up with the same movie, TV show, or music group or performer in a given round, one of those people must change the selection. Just make it fair. If you change one time, then you shouldn't have to change the next time.

OBJECTIVE

Players are challenged to come up with clues for specific movies, TV shows, and music groups which would only be recognized by as few members of the group as possible.

GAME TIME

Once everyone has written down their selections and is holding them out in full view, Player 1 makes his choices. Player 1 decides which three items he is going to give clues about for his round. He writes down those three items in the order in which he will play them on a piece of paper and doesn't let anyone see his three selections. His paper should look something like this:

1. *Shawshank Redemption*
2. *Modern Family*
3. Bruce Springsteen

> **IMPORTANT:** Player 1's three items could also look like this:

1. *Shawshank Redemption*
2. *Modern Family*
3. *Shawshank Redemption*

That's right! You can actually put the same selection in two different spots. You can even use the same selection in ALL THREE SPOTS! (See the Tip on the next page for information on why you would do that).

Player 1 must now give clues about his three selections one at a time while everyone writes down which movie, TV show, or music group they think Player 1 picked in each of his three spots. When giving clues, Player 1 must announce which item the other players should be guessing (e.g., "Here is my clue for the first item . . .") and then say something about that item that he hopes ONLY the person who wrote it on his or her card would know or recognize. This could be a line from the movie, an actor he thinks only he and that person know was in the movie, or even something about the movie that few people know. Length does not matter.

NOTE: The clue must be something about the selection. It cannot be something personal between the clue-giver and the player who wrote the selection.

Once Player 1 is done with his statement about his first selection, the other players then take 30 seconds to guess which item the clue referred to and write down their guesses. Player 1's objective is to give clues that will help the person who came up with each selection—and ONLY that person—to figure out that he picked his or her movie, TV show, or music group without revealing the item to the other players.

Player 1 then moves on and makes a statement about his second selection, again beginning by announcing which item the other players are guessing ("Here is what I have to say about my second selection . . .") Players write down their guesses for his second selection. Player 1 repeats this process for his third selection.

Once all of the players have written down their guesses for Player 1's third selection, players reveal their guesses for all three selections at once and tally points.

Play continues when all players come up with new items they think would be familiar to Player 2, and Player 2 chooses three.

TIP: There are two main reasons you may choose to give a clue for the same movie, TV show, or music group or performer in more than one of the three spots. For one, you may not know the other entertainment choices provided that well or you may not be able to come up with strong enough clues for them. Second, depending on the current point status of all the players in the game, you may not want to give certain people the chance to earn additional points by selecting their items for your round.

SCORING

SCORING FOR GUESSERS: Each player who guesses correctly on all three of Player 1's selections earns 20 points. Each player who guesses correctly on two of Player 1's three selections earns 5 points. No points if you only guessed correctly on one or none. However, if Player 1 selected YOUR item for one of the three spots, you earn 25 points if you figured it out and guessed correctly. You can actually earn an additional 75 points if Player 1 selected your item for all three spots. In that specific scenario, if you figured out all three were your item, your total for that round would be 95 points.

SCORING FOR PLAYER 1 (THE CLUE GIVER): Player 1 loses 20 points for every person who guesses correctly on all three of his or her selections. Player 1 loses 5 points for every person who guesses two of his three selections correctly. So, with 8 total players, if 4 guessed correctly on all three and 1 guessed correctly on two of the three, Player 1 (The clue giver) would lose 85 points. Player 1 doesn't lose any points if players guess correctly on one or none of the three items.

Finally, for each of the three items selected, Player 1 earns 25 points when the player who submitted the item guesses correctly that Player 1 selected his item.

Therefore, you can earn a maximum of 75 points each time it is your turn to select items and be the clue giver. It is then simply a matter of how many of your selections everyone else figures out, which determines how many points you lose.

EXAMPLE

Let's say that Player 1 created his list as follows:

1. *Shawshank Redemption*
2. *Modern Family*
3. Bruce Springsteen

For his first clue, referring to *Shawshank Redemption*, Player 1 might say, "Brooks was here," which is a line from the movie that he feels only a real fan (i.e., the person who submitted *Shawshank Redemption*) would know or remember. If Player 2 was the one who originally submitted *Shawshank Redemption* and she figured out that Player 1 was talking about her movie for the first selection, she and Player 1 would both earn 25 points. Same goes for the players who had *Modern Family* and Bruce Springsteen. If they guessed Player 1 was talking about their selections in those two spots, they would each receive 25 points and Player 1 would earn another 50 points for those two combined. So in this scenario Player 1 now has 75 points. However, two of the players in the group figured out all three of the clues. They each get 20 and Player 1 loses 40 points (20 X 2). One of the players in the group figured out two of the three clues. That player gets 5 and Player 1 loses 5. Therefore, the total for Player 1 in this round as clue giver ends up being +30 (75 minus 45).

GREED

GOOD CLUES AND KNOWING WHEN TO QUIT WILL GET YOU FAR IN THIS GAME!

PREPARATION

Each player writes down approximately twenty common, one-word objects (*hammer, television, ear, toaster, camera, computer, iron, bottle, jar, lime, lobster, brick*, etc.) on different, small pieces of paper. No names or proper nouns! These are the game pieces that are all placed together in a hat or other object, which prevents anyone from seeing them.

OBJECTIVE

Players must come up with the best possible clues to earn significant points . . . and know when to quit when someone else is giving the clues!

GAME TIME

Player 1 goes first and picks a word out of the hat without revealing it to anyone. He then gives a two-word clue for everyone to guess the word. Player 1 cannot use any part of the word in any of the two words of the clue. He can't point to anything or use any hand gestures, and he can't say the word in a foreign language.

IMPORTANT: Once Player 1 picks the one-word object out of the hat, he must say the two-word clue and NOTHING ELSE until the guesses are revealed! For example, if the word is *nose*, Player 1 could say "Smell with" as the two-word clue. Each player then writes down what he or she thinks the word is, and everyone reveals their answers at once.

Each player who gets it correct then has a choice: he or she can either "Move on" or "Stop." Those who "Stop" get to keep their points (see "Scoring"), but they cannot earn any more for that round. Those who move on can earn more points, but they also risk losing all the points they have earned. (Player 1 also earns and loses points as the other players guess, so he must try to give the best possible clues to avoid losing points.)

When the other players have made their choice, Player 1 then picks out another word and prepares a two-word clue for those who elected to move on.

IMPORTANT: Once a word is picked out of the hat, it must be discarded. Also, if a word selected from the hat has already been used in the game (more than one person submitted *chair*, for example), toss it away and pick again. The same word cannot be used twice.

Player 1 must continue until all players have either declared "Stop" or guessed incorrectly and lost their points. When the scores from Player 1's round have been tallied, Player 2 chooses a word and begins giving clues and so on until all players have had a chance to lead a round.

SCORING

When a player elects to stop, that player and Player 1 multiply the number of words he or she guessed correctly by 10, and both that player and Player 1 earn those points for the round.

If a player guesses incorrectly, both that player and Player 1 lose 10 points per word guessed—even if the previous guesses were correct. Players who get the first word wrong lose 10 points and immediately cost Player 1 10 points as well.

EXAMPLE

If Player 2 guessed six of the words correctly and then declared "Stop," she and Player 1 would both earn 60 points. If Player 3 elected to go for a seventh word and he got it wrong, both Player 3 and Player 1 would lose 70 points each—even though his first six guesses were correct.

> **TIP:** As you see, if a lot of players get too greedy when it is your round to give clues, those players will all lose points, but YOU will lose a lot more! You can set a ten-word maximum per person per round to prevent any players from getting too greedy.

UNLOCK THE SAFE

FIGURE OUT THE COMBINATION AND WIN BIG!

PREPARATION

Each player makes a list of all the players in the game with room next to each player's name to write a number.

One player writes numbers 1 through 25 on slips of paper and place them in a hat. Each player picks a number out of the hat without showing anyone the number he or she picked.

Each player must now think of a clue to help the other players decipher his number. Once every player decides on the clue he or she is going to present, play begins.

OBJECTIVE

Players must come up with a clue they think most—but not all—players in the game will figure out and must guess all numbers correctly to unlock the safe and receive important bonus points.

GAME TIME

Player 1 goes first and gives a clue about his number. All players write down their guesses next to Player 1's name on their sheet, and then Player 2 gives her clue. Play continues this way until all players have given a clue for their number and everyone has a guess for every player.

> **TIP:** Your code can be anything! Say the number in another language. Come up with a math equation and say it relatively fast so most will get it but at least one person will miss it. Say a famous athlete who wore that number on his or her jersey. Or perhaps don't use any words at all and scratch your head twenty-four times. Use any method you can think of to get at least one of the players to figure out your number (hopefully several) and to fool at least one player.

Once the final player presents the clue for his or her number and all guesses are written down, players reveal their actual numbers one at a time and scores are tallied.

SCORING

Players earn 20 points for each number they guess correctly. Players also earn 10 points for each player who guesses their number correctly. However, if EVERYONE in the game guesses a player's number correctly, that player LOSES 10 points per player in the game. And if no one guesses that player's number correctly, he or she also loses 10 points per player in the game!

EXAMPLE

Let's say Player 1's number is 24. His clue might be "The letter X." Everyone then writes down their guesses next to Player 1's name. Then Player 2 presents her clue to the group. Let's say her number is 11 and her clue is "The number of players on the field at one time for each team in football." The other players write down their guesses next to Player 2's name, and so on.

Most people in the group may figure out that the letter *X* is the 24th letter of the alphabet, and if EVERYONE gets it right, Player 1 loses 10 points per player in the game! If there are a total of 6 players in the game (including Player 1), Player 1 would lose 60 points while everyone else receives 20 points each! Player 2's clue was tougher, though, and if two of the six players could not guess the number (maybe because they don't know anything about football), she would earn 30 points (10 for each of the players who guessed correctly).

BONUS POINTS FOR THE CORRECT SAFE COMBINATION

After all numbers are revealed for every player and points are tallied, bonus points are awarded to every player who guessed every number right and holds the answer to the safe combination! The number of bonus points players receive is equivalent to 10 times the number of players in the game.

For example, in a game of six players, if three players guessed Player 1's number correctly, he'd earn 30 points (10 X 3). If Player 1 guessed correctly on all five of the other player's numbers, he'd earn 100 points (20 X 5). In addition, Player 1 would earn 60 bonus points (10 X 6 players in the game). Player 1's grand total would be 190 points.

FIND ALL THREE!

HAVE FUN WITH A STORY ABOUT PEOPLE IN YOUR GROUP.

PREPARATION

Each player has the task of making up a story about two people in the group. Choose any two people. The story should really only be one or two sentences and must be no more than thirty words long.

> **IMPORTANT:** The story cannot be something personal between two people in the group or a private joke that only a few people in the group know about. It should simply be a fresh, made-up story.

Once each player has written his or her story down, each player must choose three of the words from the story and cross out every letter but the first.

OBJECTIVE

Players take turns telling their made-up stories while the other players figure out the missing words in each story.

GAME TIME

Starting with Player 1, players take turns telling their stories. When players read their story to the group, they can only say the first letter of the three words they crossed out. The rest of the group will have to figure out what those words are.

Make the story as silly and fun as you like, but keep in mind the scoring.

SCORING

Players who are guessing the words earn 20 points if they get all three words right. They earn no points if they get even one word wrong.

The storyteller earns 50 total points if ONLY ONE player gets all three right. However, the storyteller loses 50 points if either everyone or no one guesses correctly. He or she earns 10 total points if more than one person gets it right.

> **TIP:** The challenge of figuring out your three words can't be too easy or too difficult! In either of those cases, you stand to lose a lot of points! For the maximum amount of points, you want only one person to figure it out.

EXAMPLE

Player 1's story might go something like this: "Jack and Linda drove to the s---------- to buy h--------- and hot dogs for the barbecue. While driving there, Jack realized he forgot to wear p----."

The three words missing from Player 1's sentence are *supermarket*, *hamburgers*, and *pants*. Let's say there are six players in the game. If only Player 2 guesses all three words correctly, Player 1 earns 50 points and Player 2 earns 20 points; the other players do not earn any points. If both Players 2 and 3 guess all three words correctly, then they each get 20 points and Player 1 gets only 10. If either everyone or nobody guessed all three words, Player 1 loses 50 points.

FUNNY, ODD, DISGUSTING

INDEX CARDS RECOMMENDED

A TRUE HEARING TEST AND A LOT OF CONFUSION.

PREPARATION

Each player takes a piece of paper and draws a line down the middle. On the left side, each player should make a list of three items, two words each. The first item should be someone or something funny. The second should be something odd or strange. The third should be something disgusting. Remember, each item must be exactly two words long. Players should leave the right side of the page blank to write down the other players' responses while the game is being played.

Next, players should create the "Silence Cards." These are index cards which will be handed out to every player in the game before each of the four rounds. There should be four sets of silence cards. Each set will contain a number of cards equivalent to the number of players in the game.

Three of the sets of cards will all be blank index cards. Clip each of these three sets together with a paper clip or rubber band. Before clipping the fourth set together, place an *S* on the back of every card but one, which will remain blank. Shuffle that pile well so no one will have any idea which is the blank card. Now clip that pile together as well, and then shuffle each of the four piles, keeping them face down so nobody can see the *S* pile. Then take the clips off and stack the cards on top of each other in one big pile.

OBJECTIVE

Players must attempt to identify a funny item, an odd item, and a disgusting item from three different players.

GAME TIME

Before each round, players each take one card from the top of the pile without showing anyone what they picked. Each player looks at the back of his or her card privately. If players have a blank card, they will proceed as normal. If a player has an *S* on his or her card, he or she must remain silent for that round.

For the first round, each player has the choice of saying one of his three items out loud. It doesn't matter which—funny, odd, or disgusting. At the count of three, all players say their two-word items aloud at the same time.

IMPORTANT: In this game, you want people to hear your item, so say it loud . . . but you also want to hear the other items being said at the same time.

Once players are done shouting their items, they write down, on the right side of the page, any items they heard from the other players.

TIP: If you managed to recognize who said what, then put that down next to the items as well. Most of the time, you may be able to focus on only one other player, but there's certainly a chance you will hear more.

Round two begins when players each take another card from the pile. Again, if players don't have an *S* on the back of their card, they must shout out the next item at the count of three with everyone else. There are four rounds, so players must shout out each item at least once.

IMPORTANT: Once the *S* cards come out, whichever round it happens to be, there's no reason to select cards from the pile in the following rounds.

NOTE: If you are the unlucky one to NOT get an *S* card in all four rounds, you will be shouting one of your items twice . . . and for one of those times, it will be ALL BY YOURSELF while everyone listens and chuckles.

At the end of the four rounds, players must choose and circle three items as their final guesses. From the items heard in the four rounds, players guess one item from each type: one funny, one odd, and one disgusting . . . and each one should be from a different player in the game in order to earn the bonus points! Players take turns reading their guesses aloud, and the other players confirm whether the guesses were correct in order to tally the points.

SCORING

Players earn 1 point for guessing an item correctly as long as he or she identifies the correct category and the specific player from whom it came. A player also gets 1 point every time another player guesses his or her item correctly. (For example, if Player 1 guessed that Player 2 had *Moldy cheese* as her disgusting item, but Player 2 actually had it as her odd item, neither player earns any points.)

NOTE: If two people manage to come up with the same item for any of the types, then the guesser gets to choose which player he or she wants to go with for that item. Both the guesser and the player who shouted the word get 1 point for a correct match . . . but players do not earn bonus points if they have more than one item from the same person or if they have two items of the same type.

BONUS POINTS

If your three selected items were from three different players and the three different categories (funny, odd, and disgusting), you get bonus points. That number is equivalent to the total number of players in the game. So, with seven total players in the game, if you achieve the bonus objective, you get seven extra points!

NOTE: The player who shouted his or her item out in complete silence has a point advantage ONLY for that item since everyone will most likely pick that one item. However, most people won't even listen to him or her after that, knowing that they can't pick any more of that player's items if they want to earn the bonus points. In addition, the other players have another advantage over that player for bonus points since they are all one step closer to having three different types.

READY, SET, GO!

These games are all about speed. Be the first to come up with the answer, and you win! Some of these games don't even require paper and pens and are great for passing the time on long road trips.

RELATIVES

BE THE FASTEST TO FIGURE OUT THE COMMON THEME IN THIS EXCITING TEAM CHALLENGE!

PREPARATION

First, divide the group into two teams. For each round, all players must come up with a "four-word relative," that is, four words that are all related in some way. (For example, one four-word relative could be *toast, fries, onion soup*, and *horn*. Can you guess the relationship?)

Each of the four words are clues provided one at a time to the other players as they try to find the relation of those words to a specific theme. (In the above case, that theme is "things that are French"!) Players should not let any other players, whether on their team or the other team, see their words.

> **IMPORTANT:** When creating your order of clues, the first and second clues shouldn't give it away easily, but the answer should still be possible to figure out with some creative thinking!

OBJECTIVE

Players must figure out the theme before the other team! For each round, the faster a player gets it, the more points his or her team receives.

GAME TIME

Players from each team take turns providing clues to their four-word relatives while both teams attempt to guess the theme. Player 1 goes first, giving clues one at a time. Players have 30 seconds to guess the theme for each clue. Only one guess per team per clue!

> **TIP:** This game is played Family Feud style. The first player on either team to raise his or her hand after each clue gets one guess. If that person gets the theme wrong in that one guess, the other team has 30 seconds to get together and provide one guess collectively, and so on.

The first team to guess the theme earns points (see "Scoring"). Then Player 2 gives clues for her four-word relative, and so on.

SCORING

Teams earn 20 points for guessing the theme after the first clue, 15 points for guessing after the second, 10 points for guessing after the third, and 5 points for guessing after the fourth clue.

EXAMPLES OF RELATIVES

- king, queen, twin, bunk—types of beds
- Oklahoma, Mississippi, Sacramento, concentration—words with four syllables

- river, check, call, raise—poker terms
- Jack, Cliff, Will, Bob—first names with other meanings
- B12, A1, B1, C7—gates at the airport
- John, Pete, Keith, Roger—original members of The Who
- push, pull, lift, curl—things you do with weights
- contract, jersey, check, cast—things you sign
- bone, off, rex, cup—things that go with t
- bra, belt, clothespin, sling—things that hold other things up
- lions, tigers, pistons, automobiles—Detroit
- Bill Murray, Demi Moore, Dan Aykroyd, Patrick Swayze—ghost movie actors
- Jason, Julia, Michael, Jerry—*Seinfeld* actors
- Alaska, Argentina, Alabama, Aida—begin and end with the letter a
- raise arms, stand up, put arms down, sit down—how to do the wave
- Rabbit, Beetle, Mustang, Taurus—car models
- "Girl," "Michelle," "Yesterday," "Help"—Beatles songs
- *Glory, Hard Rain, Amistad, Unforgiven*—Morgan Freeman movies
- chance, income tax, Oriental, Park Place—Monopoly
- emergency, dark, bath, living—rooms
- pit, chair, rest, wrestle—arm stuff
- balloon, cookbook, tattoo, assassin—words with two sets of double letters

- paint, men, group, drums—Blue Man Group
- cross, left, right, jab—boxing terms
- pro golf match, Broadway play, church, library—places where you need to be quiet

UNSCRAMBLE ME

A WORD-SCRAMBLE CHALLENGE WITH A TWIST!

PREPARATION

Player 1 comes up with a word that is between six and ten letters long and writes it down without letting anyone else see. Player 1 scrambles the word. Player 1 then removes one letter and reads the remaining scrambled letters out loud. The other players write the letters down.

> **NOTE:** Plural words are not permitted. In other words, *bicycle* is fine, but not *bicycles*.

OBJECTIVE

Players attempt to guess first the missing letter and then the entire word from a list of scrambled letters.

GAME TIME

Player 1 announces the word's category. The category should be fairly specific, such as *animal, US city, food*, or *sport*. The more specific the category, the faster the game will go.

The first player to figure out the word DOES NOT say the word out loud! That player only announces the MISSING LETTER. If Player 1 confirms that the missing letter is correct, then the rest of the players add that letter and compete to figure out the word.

IMPORTANT: The player who said the correct missing letter must be silent and not provide any hint for the rest of the players who are trying to figure out the word.

Play continues as players take turns presenting their scrambled words to the group.

SCORING

The player who first correctly guesses the missing letter earns 2 points. The rest of the players then compete to be the first to figure out the entire word for 1 point. However, if the player who guessed the missing letter guesses incorrectly, Player 1 must reveal the correct letter, and the other players then have the chance to earn 2 points for guessing the correct word.

IMPORTANT: When a player guesses the missing letter incorrectly, that player DOES NOT get to compete for the two points!

EXAMPLE

Let's say Player 1 says, "My scrambled word is R-A-N-O-K-A-O, and the category is *animal*." Then Player 2 figures out that the word is *kangaroo* and the missing letter is G. Player 2 says, "The missing letter is G." Player 1 says, "Correct," and Player 2 earns 2 points. The rest of the players now know that the scrambled letters of the complete word are *R, A, N, O, K, A, O*, and *G*. If Player 4 is the first to say "Kangaroo," Player 4 would earn 1 point.

TIP: You can make this game more challenging by not allowing any writing or by increasing the word length.

BACKWARDS PEOPLE

A REVERSE EXPERIENCE!

Players take turns coming up with known people (famous people or people everyone in the game knows). Pronounce the name backwards . . . first name, then last!

TIP: It is much easier if you write the first and last name down backwards from right to left so you can look at it before you pronounce it.

Players guessing cannot write down what they hear. (That's way too easy!) The first player to guess the name earns 1 point.

EXAMPLES

NHOJ/ATLOVART . . . YTTEB/SIVAD . . . ODRANOEL/OIR-PACID . . . AIRAM/AVOPARAHS

ANSWERS: John Travolta, Betty Davis, Leonardo Di-Caprio, Maria Sharapova

I SEE YOU!

LOOK CAREFULLY. THE WORD WILL REVEAL ITSELF EVENTUALLY!

PREPARATION

Each player thinks of a seven- to ten-letter word. Without showing anyone, players write the word down with spaces in between the letters in order to place ten other random letters in between the letters in the word.

A word such as *computer* would look something like this:

CLKAOMURPUSYOTIEAR

(The letters of the word *computer* are only underlined for this example to show you where it is in the long line of letters.)

OBJECTIVE

Players attempt to be the first to find the hidden word!

GAME TIME

Player 1 goes first and reads his long list of letters from left to right so everyone can write them down. Players begin to try and find the word and guess what it is. Every 20 seconds, Player 1 tells the other players to cross out a specific letter (one of the letters which is not in the word). Using the above example, he may say things like "Cross out the *K*" or "Cross out the first *A*" or "Cross out the last *O*." The first person to guess the word wins the round and earns points (see "Scoring").

Player 2 then reads her list of letters, and so on.

SCORING

The sooner a player guesses the word, the more points he or she earns. If a player guesses the word before Player 1 crosses off the first letter, he or she earns 100 points. For every letter Player 1 crosses off, players earn 10 points less (subtracting from 100). (For example, if you guess the word after Player 1 crosses off four letters, you earn 60 points.) The first player to 500 points wins!

TWINS

IT'S A RACE TO FIND THE PAIR!

PREPARATION

Each player thinks of two words which have something in common, such as *baseball* and *basketball, trumpet* and *trombone, airport* and *terminal*, etc. No plurals allowed! Players draw dashes in a line representing the number of letters in the two words if they were placed next to each other. (For example, with *baseball* and *basketball*, the total number of letters in both words combined is eighteen: *baseballbasketball*.

OBJECTIVE

Players attempt to be the first to find the pair.

GAME TIME & EXAMPLE

Using the example of *baseball* and *basketball*, Player 1 goes first and tells the other players to draw eighteen dashes. Player 1 then tells everyone to place specific letters one at a time over specific dashes. Every 15 seconds, he provides one letter until someone shouts out what he or she thinks the two words are. However, Player 1 must provide the letter clues in the following sequence:

1. First letter of the first word.
2. Last letter of the second word.
3. Second letter of the first word.
4. Second-to-last letter of the second word.
5. Third letter of the first word . . . and so on.

After seven letters are placed with the example of *baseballbasketball*, the line should look like this:

base_ _ _ _ _ _ _ _ _ _ _ _all

Play continues as players take turns coming up with "twin" words.

SCORING

The first player to figure out the two words and shout out the correct answer earns 5 points for that round. HOWEVER, if players guess incorrectly, they are out of the round (only one guess per player per round). In addition, each time a player shouts out a wrong guess, the prize for the correct answer increases by 5 points for the rest of the players competing. The first player to earn 100 points wins!

ADD 'EM UP!

WORD MATH . . . IT'S MORE FUN THAN IT SOUNDS.

PREPARATION

Draw a chart on a piece of paper with all of the letters of the alphabet corresponding to a number from 1 to 26 (A=1, B=2, C=3, and so on to Z=26), and place it on the table so all players can see it.

OBJECTIVE

Players attempt to come up with more words than everyone else in each round!

GAME TIME

Player 1 goes first and picks whether the challenge will be 3-, 4-, or 5-letter words. Player 2 then picks one letter which must be used as the first letter of each word. Player 3 then decides on a ten-point range which must be achieved.

> **NOTE:** Three-letter words should be within 10–60 points. Four-letter words should be within 20–75 points. Five-letter words should be within 30–90 points.

Player 1 sets a 5-minute timer, and all at once, each player must try to come up with as many words as possible that meet the chosen criteria (length, starting letter, and point range). When time is up, players tally their points, and the next round begins with Player 2 selecting the number of letters in the words, Player 3 choosing a starting letter, and Player 4 selecting a specific 10-point range. The round after that, Player 3 selects the number of letters in the word, Player 4 chooses a starting letter, and so on.

SCORING

Regardless of the length of each word, players earn one point per word that meets all three criteria. The number of correct words players come up with is the number of points they receive for that round.

EXAMPLE

Let's say Player 1 picks five-letter words; Player 2 says the letter *C* must be the first letter; Player 3 says the points should be between 41 and 50. (You can choose any 10-point range, but we advise that you stay within the guidelines listed above according to the total number of letters being used.) Once the timer starts, every player tries to come up with as many five-letter words as possible that begin with the letter *C* that will be worth between 41 and 50 points. (The word *crush* has a total of 69 points, so it would not make the list: C=3, R=18, U=21, S=19, and H=8. The word *clamp*, however, has a total of 45 points (C=3, L=12, A=1, M=13, and P=16), so the player would receive a point for that word.

THAT'S ENTERTAINMENT

THIS SPEEDY CHALLENGE IS PERFECT FOR FANS OF POP CULTURE.

PREPARATION

Player 1 thinks of an actor and a movie and gives a three-letter clue. The first two are the first letters of the actor's first and last names; the third letter is the first letter of the title of a movie he or she starred in.

> **TIP:** Be sure to leave the articles (*the, a, an*) out of the movie titles.

OBJECTIVE

Players attempt to be the first to guess the actor and movie, singer and band, author and book, etc.

GAME TIME (ACTORS AND MOVIES)

Players have 60 seconds to guess the actor and movie based solely on the three letters. If no one can guess it within 60

seconds, players take turns asking for additional clues, such as, "Give us the second letter of the actor's first name" or "Give us the second letter of the movie title." The first player to guess the actor and the movie wins the round and receives points (see "Scoring").

Player 2 now thinks of an actor and a movie, gives a three-letter clue, and so on.

SCORING

If a player guesses correctly in the first 60 seconds, he or she earns 10 points. After each additional clue, subtract 2 points from 10. (In other words, if someone guesses the actor and movie correctly after one clue, that player earns 8 points; after two clues, 6 points; three clues, 4 points; four clues, 2 points.) Players can earn only 1 point after more than four clues have been given. The first player to earn 50 points wins!

EXAMPLES

- APS; Answer: Al Pacino, *Scarface*
- TCM; Answer: Tom Cruise, *Mission Impossible*
- WFA; Answer: Will Ferrell, *Anchorman*

WHAT'S MY FOUR-LETTER WORD?

BE THE FASTEST TO GUESS THE FOUR-LETTER WORD WITHOUT ANY WRITING!

OBJECTIVE

Players take turns giving clues for their four-letter words and try to be the first to guess the other players' words.

GAME TIME

Player 1 thinks of a four-letter word and then comes up with four three-letter words which are clues to figuring out the four-letter word. Each three-letter word must contain one letter that is in the four-letter word. No writing allowed!

> **NOTE:** The three-letter words don't have to have anything to do with the four-letter word. The only requirement is that each of them contain one of the letters found in the four-letter word.

Player 1 gives the three-letter words in order, with the first letter of the four-letter word somewhere in the first clue, the second letter of the four-letter word somewhere in the second clue, and so on. The first player to guess the four-letter word wins the round and earns 1 point.

Play continues as Player 2 gives clues for her four-letter word, and so on.

SCORING (6+ PLAYERS)

With six or more players, players earn 1 point for guessing a four-letter word correctly, and the first player to earn 5 points wins.

SCORING (LESS THAN 6 PLAYERS)

With 3–5 players, the first player to earn 3 points wins. However, players who aren't the first person to guess the word lose 1 point each time!

For example, if Player 4 guesses the first word from Player 1, she gets 1 point. If she guesses the next one from Player 2, she gets another point for a total of 2. She can now win the game with three points if she is the first to guess the next one from Player 3. However, if Player 5 guesses the next one from Player 3, then Player 5 gets 1 point and Player 4 loses a point and goes back to 1. If Player 2 guesses the next one, then both Player 4 and Player 5 go back to 0. (Players never go into negative points, though; they just stay at zero.)

IMPORTANT: When it is your turn to come up with a four-letter word and give clues, your current points freeze until after your turn.

EXAMPLES

Four-Letter Word: *prom*; **Clues:** *pig, art, old, arm*
Four-Letter Word: *flag*; **Clues:** *off, lot, bar, rug*
Four-Letter Word: *jump*; **Clues:** *jog, mud, ham, tap*

DON'T TELL FRANK HE'S GOING BALD!

HANGMAN MEETS WHEEL OF FORTUNE . . . AND IT'S PERSONAL.

PREPARATION

Each player puts together a five- to seven-word sentence about someone else in the game without revealing the sentence to the other players.

> **NOTE:** The sentence can be about anyone, and it certainly doesn't have to be a true statement.

OBJECTIVE

Players attempt to be the first to guess the sentence.

GAME TIME & EXAMPLE

Player 1 begins by telling the other players how many words are in his sentence and how many letters are in each word. On their own sheets of paper, the other players draw dashes representing the letters in each word of the sentence. Then everyone places numbers under each dash from left to right, starting with 1 as the first letter of the first word, 2 as the second letter of the first word, etc. (Spaces and punctuation don't count.) If there are only three letters in the first word, then the number 4 would be the first letter of the second word, and so on.

The phrase "Don't tell Frank he's going bald" would look like this:

_ _ _ ' _ / _ _ _ _ / _ _ _ _ _ / _ _ ' _ /
1 2 3 4 5 6 7 8 9 10 11 12 13 14 15 16

_ _ _ _ _ / _ _ _ _
17 18 19 20 21 22 23 24 25

Players take turns asking Player 1 to fill in a specific letter. If Player 2 begins by selecting *N*, Player 1 would then tell everyone where the letter *N* goes. In the above example, Player 1 would say, "*N* goes above the numbers 3, 12, and 20." If Player 3 then asks for the letter *A*, Player 1 would then say, "*A* goes in slots 11 and 23."

Players take turns asking for a letter until one player shouts out the correct sentence and wins the round. If you shout out the wrong sentence, you are out of the round and have no more guesses.

Player 2 goes next, sharing the number of words in her sentence and the number of letters in each word, and so on.

SCORING

A player wins one point for every phrase he or she guesses correctly. The person with the most correct guesses after everyone takes a turn with his or her phrase wins.

DUCK DRUM DOLPHIN DAISY DRAGON

THE SECRET LIES IN ONE COMMON LETTER.

PREPARATION

Each player comes up with his or her own list of five one-word common objects or things without revealing the list to the other players. No names allowed! All five words must begin with the same letter. (For example, Player 1's list might be *duck, drum, dolphin, daisy, dragon.*) The player choosing the words should NOT reveal his or her starting letter.

OBJECTIVE

Players must guess as many words as they can before anyone else!

GAME TIME

Player 1 begins by telling the other players how many letters are in each word. On their own sheets of paper, the other players draw dashes representing the letters in each of the five words. Then everyone places numbers under each dash from left to right, starting with 1 as the first letter of the first word, 2 as the second letter of the first word, etc. (Spaces and punctuation don't count.) If there are only three letters in the first word, then the number 4 would be the first letter of the second word, and so on.

The words *duck, drum, dolphin, daisy, dragon* would look like this:

_ _ _ _ / _ _ _ _ / _ _ _ _ _ _ _ /

1 2 3 4 5 6 7 8 9 10 11 12 13 14 15

_ _ _ _ _ / _ _ _ _ _ _

16 17 18 19 20 21 22 23 24 25 26

The player to the left of Player 1 writes down a letter on a separate piece of paper and shows it ONLY to Player 1. Without revealing the letter to the other players, Player 1 says out loud where that letter fits in all five words. (For instance, if someone showed Player 1 the letter *O* in the above example, Player 1 would say, "That letter is 10 and 25.") The player who asked for the letter knows exactly what letter is in those two spots, but the other players only know that those two spots contain the same letter.

Players take turns asking for a letter secretly. When players think they have figured out one of the words, they raise their hand. Player 1 asks that player which word and to say his or her answer out loud. If the player is correct, he or she earns points for guessing it before anyone else. If he or she is wrong, that player cannot guess again for that specific word!

(Player 1 writes down players' names next to words they cannot guess again.) Only one guess per word per player. Players keep guessing until all five words are found and scores are tallied (see "Scoring").

Player 2 then chooses five words that begin with the same letter and tells the other players how many letters are in each of her words, and so on.

SCORING

Players earn 5 points for guessing a word correctly. Tally the scores from each player's set of words to find a grand total and an overall winner.

TRY TO REMEMBER

Here are seven fun games to test your memory. How well can you remember what you have seen or heard? What kind of memory techniques can you use to get a leg up on your competition?

THE SECRET WORD

WHAT DID THEY SAY? WHAT DIDN'T THEY SAY? GET THEM ALL RIGHT, AND WIN BIG!

PREPARATION

Each player needs three sheets of paper. On the first, players must come up with a list of seven words that sound alike or rhyme, such as *tire, hire, buyer, fire, liar, wire*, and *sire*.

> **NOTE:** You may not place two words on your list that are pronounced the same but spelled differently such as *break* and *brake* or *maid* and *made*.

Players make a list from 1 to 8 going down the page. Players write their seven words anywhere on the list, leaving one number blank. (In other words, you can place three of your words next to 1, 2, and 3, leave 4 blank, and then place the other four words next to 5, 6, 7, and 8.)

> **IMPORTANT:** Write your words down clearly so they can eventually be read by all the other players without issue.

Next to the number left blank, players write the words "MY PHRASE" in all caps. (Later on, when that number comes up, each player will have to say a three-word phrase.)

On a second sheet of paper, players make another list of three items: the "secret word" list. To create this list, players pick one of the words from the original list to be their "secret word." Players circle that word on the original list and write that word at the top of the second list with *secret word* next to it. Next, players must come up with another word that doesn't rhyme with the words on their original list, a "replacement" word. Players write that word beneath the secret word and write *replacement word* next to it. Under that, players write a three-word phrase. Make the phrase something fun, but keep it simple so that people can easily remember and know how to spell it. (*I'll be back* or *My feet stink* or *Bob loves Megan* would all be acceptable three-word phrases.)

> **IMPORTANT:** Never show your secret word list to anyone. In fact, while you are playing, make sure nobody can see either list you have made until it is time to share your main list.

On a third sheet of paper, players list the names of all the other players in the game with room to write two words and one three-word phrase next to each name. Set this sheet aside until all the lists have been read.

OBJECTIVE

Players must identify the other players' secret words while also remembering their replacement words and their three-word phrases.

GAME TIME

Player 1 begins by reading the first word on his original list out loud. Then Player 2 reads the first word on her list out loud, and the remaining players take turns reading all of the words in the order they have them listed from 1 to 8. However, when the secret word comes up on a player's list, he or she should read the replacement word instead.

IMPORTANT: Never say your secret word out loud!

In addition, when the three-word phrase comes up, players should say their three-word phrase.

TIP: After reading a word or phrase, players should circle it to ensure they do not read it again. (When you say your "replacement word," there will be nothing for you to circle since that is the word which will replace your secret word, which is already circled. You can simply pretend to circle it once you say it.)

IMPORTANT: During the process of everyone reading their lists, you may circle words ONLY AS YOU READ THEM. You are not allowed to take notes or write anything else!

All in all, every player in the game will be required to read seven words and one phrase out loud: the six words that rhyme with the secret word, the one replacement word, and the three-word phrase.

When players are done reading everything on their main lists, all of the words and the phrase should now be circled. Now each player should pull out the list he or she made of all the other player's names. The lists of rhyming words are then passed around the table. When players receive another player's list, they must write down on their third piece of paper next to that player's name (1) his or her secret word, (2) what they remember being his replacement word, and (3) his three-word phrase.

NOTE: Only one of those three things will be on the player's list: his or her secret word! The other two you will simply have to remember without any visual aid.

SCORING

Once all players have their written guesses down, all answers are revealed. Players earn 3 points for every secret word they guess correctly, 3 points for every replacement word they guess correctly, and 3 points for every three-word phrase they remembered.

TRIFECTA BONUS POINTS

If a player correctly guesses/remembers all three items from a specific player, he or she receives 5 bonus points!

SAMPLE:

Sally
1) spike
2) hike
3) MY PHRASE
4) like
5) Mike
6) pike
7) bike
8) lke
Sally's Secret Word List
Secret Word: bike
Replacement Word: rich
Phrase: Bob loves Megan.

WHERE'S JOHN KEEPING HIS TUBA?

INTERESTING PEOPLE PUTTING FUN THINGS IN STRANGE PLACES.

PREPARATION

Each player draws a grid with three columns and three rows for a total of nine boxes. Players number their boxes from 1 to 3 down the left side and from A to C along the top from left to right. In each box, players should write the numbers 1, 2, and 3 vertically down, leaving space to write three different words in each box.

Player 1 is the first to fill in his twenty-seven spaces. Going around the room beginning with Player 2, each player names a person, then a thing, and then a location. (For example, Player 2 starts and names a person, then Player 3 names a thing, and then Player 4 names a location. Player 5 starts again with a person, then Player 6 names a thing, and so on.) When it comes back around to Player 2, she continues in the order of where the last player left off. (Player 1 does not contribute in naming people, things, or places.)

Every time someone says something, Player 1 must write it in one of the boxes. He must put all the people on line 1 of a box, all the things on line 2 of a box, and all the places on line 3 of a box. Player 1 does this until all twenty-seven items have been placed. Player 1 can and should mix them all up so the other players won't have any idea where all of the people, things, and places have been positioned in his grid.

TIP: Go slowly enough around the room so that Player 1 has the chance to write everything down.

NOTE: So what counts as a "person"? You can name any person in the game, of course, or any well-known person or character all players are familiar with. What counts as a "thing"? Anything, really! It could even be a pet (though some people might be more inclined to put their pets under the "people" category). The sillier you make it, the better, but the sky is the limit. Finally, what counts as a "location"? Well, you could go with a city, state, or country, a typical location like *the park*, or more obscure places like *in between my teeth* or *under the sink* or *in Bob's hairpiece*.

OBJECTIVE

Players must remember what the other players say when going around the room and try to determine *who* placed *what* and *where*.

GAME TIME

Once Player 1 fills in his grid with items in all twenty-seven slots, Player 2 begins by calling out a grid location, such as "A1" or "B3" or "C2." Player 1 must now look at the grid and ask a question that corresponds with that grid location.

For all of the grid locations in row 1, Player 1 must structure his questions to leave out the "locations" from line 3. (For example, for box A1, if *John* and *tuba* were items 1 and

2 in the chosen box, Player 1 would ask, "Where did John put his tuba?" Or, if *Lady Gaga* and *chicken wings* were items 1 and 2 in the box, Player 1 would ask, "Where did Lady Gaga put her chicken wings?") Player 2 would then have to guess the location of that item based on what she remembers of all the options of places named when creating the grid.

For all of the grid locations in row 2, Player 1 must structure his questions to leave out the "things" in line 2 of each box. (For example, if *Jodie Foster* and *on Gabe's head* were lines 1 and 3 in the chosen box, Player 1 would ask, "What did Jodie Foster put on Gabe's Head?" Or, if *Abraham Lincoln* and *in Ralph's toupee* were lines 1 and 3 of the box, Player 1 would ask, "What did Abraham Lincoln put in Ralph's toupee?")

Finally, for all of the grid locations in row 3, Player 1 must structure the questions to leave out the "people" in line 1 of each box. (For example, if *bowl of pudding* and *in the toaster* were lines 2 and 3 in the chosen box, Player 1 would ask, "Who put the bowl of pudding in the toaster?" Or if *Jerry's fingernails* and *in Kelly's bed* were lines 2 and 3 in the box, Player 1 would ask, "Who put Jerry's fingernails in Kelly's bed?")

Every player picks a box and tries to guess the missing person, place, or thing. Players only get one guess to get it right; whether a player guesses correctly or incorrectly, play moves on to the next player, who chooses a new box and answers a new question. Keep going around the room as many times as necessary until all of Player 1's questions have been answered correctly.

TIP: You should be able to get them all eventually based on both process of elimination and your memories of what you all placed in the grid.

Player 2 now creates her own grid with the group, and play continues.

SCORING

Players who guess the missing item correctly earn 1 point. Player 1 puts their name or initials in that box and circles the box on his grid to keep track of the total score for each player for his or her round. The player with the most total points for all grids combined wins the game.

SAMPLE:

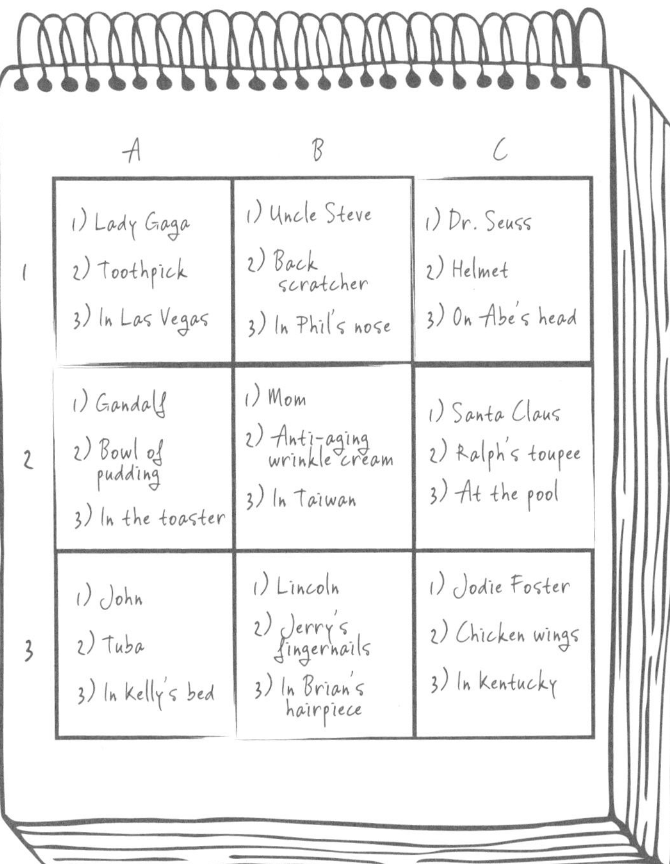

A
B
C
1
1) Lady Gaga
2) Toothpick
3) In Las Vegas
1) Uncle Steve
2) Back scratcher
3) In Phil's nose
1) Dr. Seuss
2) Helmet
3) On Abe's head
2
1) Gandalf
2) Bowl of pudding
3) In the toaster
1) Mom
2) Anti-aging wrinkle cream
3) In Taiwan
1) Santa Claus
2) Ralph's toupee
3) At the pool
3
1) John
2) Tuba
3) In Kelly's bed
1) Lincoln
2) Jerry's fingernails
3) In Brian's hairpiece
1) Jodie Foster
2) Chicken wings
3) In Kentucky

COUPLES CONCENTRATION

A FUN WAY TO PLAY THE CLASSIC GAME OF CONCENTRATION WITH A GROUP.

PREPARATION

All players create two grids of eight columns and five rows, resulting in forty boxes each, on two separate sheets of paper. Place numbers 1 through 8 along the top from left to right for the eight columns and letters A through E down the left side for the rows. In the first grid, each player places twenty "couples" somewhere in the grid. (For example, in one box you would put *Romeo*, and in another box you would put *Juliet*; in one box you would put *Bonnie*, and in another box you would put *Clyde*.)

> **TIP:** You can use couples everyone knows in your group, such as friends and family members or famous people, or you can get creative: *Bert* and *Ernie* could be a couple, or you can even go with *oil* and *vinegar*, *Star Trek* and *Star Wars*, or *shoes* and *socks*.

The second grid each player makes is a scorekeeping grid and remains blank for the time being.

OBJECTIVE

For each grid, players attempt to find more couples than everyone else.

GAME TIME

Player 1 starts the game with his grid, and the other players set their grids aside until their round. Like the card game Concentration, every player takes turns asking Player 1 to reveal who is in two specific boxes.

> **IMPORTANT:** Player 1 should not let any player see his completed game grid at any time during his round.

Player 2 goes first and asks for two boxes to be revealed by Player 1, one at a time. (For example, Player 2 may first ask for "A4," and Player 1 may reply to the group, "That's *George Washington*," and then Player 2 may ask for "C7," and Player 1 may reply to the group, "That's *Tom Cruise*. No match.") One player at a time asks Player 1 to reveal two boxes. When a player gets a match, he or she goes again, asking for two more boxes. However, if a player's guess does not turn up a match, play moves on to the next player.

To keep track of the matches and points, Player 1 uses his scorekeeping grid to write the name of the player who got the match in both boxes.

> **IMPORTANT:** The scorekeeping grid should always be in full view of all the other players. That way, all players know which matches have already been completed and can avoid asking for those specific boxes again.

Once the grid from Player 1 is completed, round two begins with a new grid from Player 2. Go around the room until all players' grids are guessed, then tally up the points for the final score.

SCORING

Players earn 1 point for every box they occupy in the scoring grid. Therefore, if a player gets eight matches, he or she will earn a total of 16 points for that round.

PASS OR NO PASS

INDEX CARDS RECOMMENDED

STUMP YOUR FRIENDS IN THIS TRUE TEST OF MEMORIZATION.

PREPARATION

Every player takes a piece of paper or index card and makes a vertical list of four three-word phrases in large lettering, numbering them from 1 to 4. Each three-word phrase in this game must include the name of someone in the game as the first word and follow the same "person, adjective, noun" pattern. Example:

1. BRIAN'S LARGE MUSTACHE
2. KELLY'S CRAZY UNCLE
3. LINDSAY'S BEAUTIFUL ARMPIT
4. ANTHONY'S AMAZING ANTEATER

Be creative and write legibly! Players can use the same person for more than one phrase or even all four, but at least one word in each three-word phrase must be different.

On the back of the card, players must write their name (also in large lettering) so nobody has to squint to see it. Each player then holds his or her card up with his or her name facing outward.

IMPORTANT: After everyone is finished writing their phrases and names, pens are down for the remainder of the game!

One at a time, beginning with Player 1, each player takes turns reading a phrase on his or her card going in order from number 1 to number 4. For example, Player 1 will read his first phrase, then Player 2 will read her first phrase, Player 3 his first phrase, and so on until it gets back to Player 1, who will read his second phrase, and everyone will follow again until every player in the game has read all four of his or her three-word phrases.

TIP: You can make this game harder or easier by having more or fewer phrases on each card.

OBJECTIVE

Players attempt to be the first to go around the room and correctly guess a phrase in the requested position from each player's list.

GAME TIME

Once all players have read their lists out loud, Player 1 goes first and picks any other player in the game. That player then asks Player 1 to recall one specific phrase from his or her card. For example, if Player 1 chooses Player 3, then Player 3 might say, "What is my number 4?" Players have only 10 seconds to answer the question each time!

If Player 1 correctly recalls the three-word phrase in the exact position of number 4 on Player 3's card, Player 3 must say "Pass" and put the card down on the table name up so no one can see his list. Player 1 then continues and picks another player, and that player (just like Player 3) asks Player 1 to come up with the three-word phrase in a specific position on his or her own card. Every time Player 1 guesses correctly, the player whose card it is says "Pass" and puts the card down on the table with the name face up like Player 3 above. Player 1 continues to go around the room until he guesses incorrectly.

When Player 1 fails to guess the correct three-word phrase from a player's card, that player says "No pass," and the two exchange cards. (For example, let's say Player 4 asked Player 1 to give her the phrase in position number 2 on her card and Player 1 guessed incorrectly. Player 4 then says "No pass" and they exchange cards.) Additionally, everyone else who previously said "Pass" to Player 1 gets to pick up their cards again and hold them name facing out.

IMPORTANT: When you say "No pass," DO NOT shout out the correct answer! The player who got it wrong will see it because you are exchanging cards, and only that player will now know for certain where he or she was stumped.

The player who said "No pass" then immediately takes his or her turn choosing other players and attempting to guess the three-word phrases in the positions requested.

Players keep exchanging cards when a wrong answer is provided. Players must ask about the card they are holding when another player calls on them, even if it isn't their original card. The name on the back will always be in full view, so the guesser knows which list he or she needs to recall when asked the question.

The first player to successfully go around the room with a "Pass" from every other player wins.

TIP: For an easy pass when you are no longer holding your own original card, you can always pick the person who is holding your original card first on your turn, but the BETTER strategy is to leave your own card for the end. No reason to remind people what any of your phrases are or where they are in your list!

IMPORTANT TWIST:

To add a fun twist, incorporate the following "wild card" option:

Every player holds one wild card per game. A wild card allows you to say "No pass" even if the player gets it right! The wild card is added to this game to essentially give everyone a chance to take at least one turn at guessing and for players to have the opportunity to prevent someone from winning the game early on when all phrases and their positions are most fresh in everyone's minds.

For example, let's say Player 1 selects Player 5, and Player 5 asks for the third phrase on his card. Player 1 guesses correctly. Player 5, however, can now use his wild card option and say "No pass!" Player 5 must now do two things: (1) He must first announce that he is using his wild card so everyone knows Player 1 in this case got it right and Player 5 has no more wild card option left. Second, Player 5 must now change the phrase in that position and tell everyone what it is!

Let's say the phrase in the number 3 position on the card Player 5 was holding is "Lindsay's beautiful armpit." Player 5 must now cross that out on the card, write the new phrase in its place (the only time you are allowed to use a pen once the guessing begins and only for this purpose), and let everyone know what the replacement phrase is. Player 5 might say something like "Lindsay's beautiful armpit" is now "Kelly's ugly elbow." He will then exchange the card with Player 1, and now Player 5 will take his turn.

SAMPLE:

1) BRIAN'S LARGE MUSTACHE
2) KELLY'S CRAZY UNCLE
3) LINDSAY'S BEAUTIFUL ARMPIT
4) ANTHONY'S AMAZING ANTEATER

KELLY

PHOTOGRAPHIC MEMORY

WHICH PICTURES WEREN'T IN THE ORIGINAL DRAWING?

PREPARATION

Each player draws a picture containing ten different objects and nothing else. The objects can be anything: an apple, a man, the sun, the moon, a nose, a candle, a box, a cat, a wizard, etc. Each object must be different, and no two objects should look alike. (In other words, each player can draw only one person, one car, one tree, one bush, and one dog, etc. The player's person shouldn't look like their dog, and their tree shouldn't look like their bush, and so on.) Draw each object anywhere on a sheet of paper. Make the objects as clear as possible (within the scope of your talents), and leave enough room for five other objects of equal size to be added to your picture later on. Players should write their own name clearly at the top of their picture.

Players should also create score cards on a separate sheet of paper. Each player should write the name of every player in the game (including their own) with the numbers 1 through

5 below each one, leaving room to create a list of five objects for each player.

OBJECTIVE

Players must find the objects that were added to all of the other pictures and make it difficult for other players to find the new objects in their own pictures.

GAME TIME

Players pass their pictures around the table. Give each player 60 seconds to study each picture.

> **NOTE:** The more players in the game, the more time you can allow for studying the pictures.

Look at all of the objects in the pictures carefully! Continue rotating the drawings until they return to the original artists. Once each paper returns to its owner, players label the ten objects in their pictures. In other words, write *dog* next to the dog, *cat* next to the cat, *apple* next to the apple, and so on. Don't show anyone your pictures while you are labeling your objects!

Now each player adds five new objects to his or her own picture. DO NOT let anyone see what you are drawing. Remember, you cannot draw an object that looks exactly like another in your picture.

Players must label each new object like the others and place the name of the object on their score card under their name. This is essentially the answer key for each player's picture. Players should put their picture on the table facedown when they are finished labeling the new objects and adding them to their score card.

Now all the pictures are passed around the table again. While looking at each picture, players should write down the five objects they feel were not in the original picture. Players must write those objects under that artist's name on their score card. Once all players are done writing down their guesses for all of the pictures, the score cards should be complete. Now, one at a time, each original artist places his or her picture face up in the center of the table and reveals which five objects were added after the first viewing. Players reveal their guesses and tally points.

SCORING

For every new object that players guess correctly on someone else's picture, they earn 1 point.

In addition, the original artist receives a point for every object that was missed by another player. (For example, if Player 2 guessed correctly on three of Player 1's five added objects, she earns 3 points and Player 1 earns 2 points for the two objects she missed.

The player with the most points after one full round wins.

SAMPLE:

TIP: You can earn a lot of extra points for your own objects from everyone in the game if you disguise them well!

TRY TO FOCUS—IT'S REALLY ALL YOU CAN DO UNDER THIS AMOUNT OF PRESSURE.

PREPARATION

Each player in the game writes twenty random words on small, separate pieces of paper and mixes them together with everyone else's words facedown on a table or in a hat where no one can see them. These are the game pieces.

OBJECTIVE

Under intense pressure, players must remember the words they select each turn.

GAME TIME

Player 1 goes first and states how many words (anywhere from one to twenty) he wants to remember. Player 2 then draws that many random pieces from the hat. Player 2 must read each word aloud slowly to Player 1. Player 1 CANNOT write the words down!

When Player 2 is done saying the specified number of words, the other players get 30 seconds to distract Player 1 by saying all sorts of other words.

IMPORTANT: Player 1 may not hold his hands over his ears or make any noise during these 30 seconds!

When time is up, Player 2 says, "Silence!" Player 1 must now repeat the words Player 2 said in any order. He has no more than 60 seconds to accomplish this.

If Player 1 remembers all the words, both Player 1 and Player 2 earn points (see "Scoring"). However, if Player 1 misses any of the words, then Player 1 and Player 2 both lose points. Player 2 now gets to choose how many words she wants to remember, and Player 3 will draw exactly that many words from the hat and read them aloud.

IMPORTANT: If Player 1 remembers all his words, Player 2 must select a number of words to remember which is greater than the number Player 1 guesses! If Player 1 misses any of the words, then Player 2 has her choice of guessing any number of words from one to twenty. That process continues for every player who follows in the round. In each round, every player must read once and remember once. Every player has two chances to EARN or LOSE points per round.

Once the last player goes, the round is over, and players begin the next round with a clean slate. All game pieces picked in round one are placed back in the hat.

NOTE: As the rounds go on, the game pieces may start to grow familiar, which gives players a chance to push the limits of their memories and attempt higher and higher numbers—with higher risk.

To make it fair, Player 2 tests her memory first in the next round. It is important to rotate on each round. Player 1 should go last in round two. Player 2 should go last in round three, and so on. In addition, players can change the person who reads the words to a given player on each round by having each person randomly pick a name out of a hat. This way, each player gets to benefit from reading to the players with the best memories in the game and vice versa.

SCORING

To determine how many points each pair of players will earn or lose, multiply the number of words remembered by itself. (For example, if Player 1 attempted and remembered five words, both he and Player 2, the player who read the list to Player 1, would earn 25 points: 5 X 5. On the other hand, if Player 1 messed up and didn't remember all five words, both he and Player 2 would LOSE 25 points!) The player reading the words always receives or loses the same amount of points as the player who succeeds or fails in remembering them.

UNCOMMON COMBOS

WELL, THAT'S SOMETHING YOU DON'T HEAR EVERY DAY!

PREPARATION

In each round of this game, every player combines two words that rarely go together (e.g., *shoe salt, iguana picnic, melon toe, egg pants, monkey cheese*, etc.) without revealing either word to the rest of the players.

IMPORTANT: No writing is allowed in this game!

OBJECTIVE

Players compete to be the first to shout out the uncommon combo when they hear the second clue.

GAME TIME & EXAMPLE

Player 1 comes up with his own definition or description for the first of his two words and says it out loud. (For example, if his two-word combination is *shoe salt*, his first description might be "You wear it on your foot" or "Sometimes it has laces.") These clues should be fairly simple. Nobody says anything after hearing the description, and no one writes anything down. After Player 1 describes his first word, Player 2 describes her first word, and so on until every player has given a definition or description for the first half of each two-word combination.

Once it rotates back to Player 1, the guessing begins. Player 1 will now give a definition or description of his second word. (For the above example, *shoe salt*, his description for *salt* might be "It goes with pepper" or "Its synonym is sodium chloride" or "A condiment you put on food to make it taste better.")

Players must attempt to guess the full word combination by deciphering the current clue for the second word and remembering the clue provided by Player 1 for the first word. If nobody guesses correctly after a certain amount of time, Player 1 continues to give new clues for both words until someone guesses the combo. Then Player 2 gives the description or definition of her second word, and so on until every two-word combo has been guessed.

Everyone comes up with new two-word combos for the next round.

SCORING

The first player to say the correct answer for a combination gets 1 point. Set a number of rounds to play, and the most total points wins.

REMEMBER: The answer is not just Player 1's second word; it is the combination. Players must remember the description of his first word and combine the two! Just giving one of the two words will not earn players any points.

I'M PUZZLED!

Here are some fun puzzles which are fairly easy to make. Each of them will require some thought, but once you get your creative juices flowing, you should have no trouble putting them together. Split your group into teams. One player from each team is given the task of creating the same type of puzzle, and the objective for all of these puzzles is the same: to be the first team to solve each puzzle!

MATCH 'EM UP!

PICK A THEME, PICK YOUR TEAMS, AND SEE WHO CAN MAKE ALL THE MATCHES.

> **TIP:** A "Match 'Em Up" game board can be created using any of several different themes. The most popular themes are typically movies, TV shows, music, sports, books, or geography, but depending on the interests of the group, there are many more possibilities. (The following description will use movies and actors.)

PREPARATION (MOVIES AND ACTORS)

The game board consists of two columns. The first column lists twenty movies, and the second lists twenty actors in random order. Each movie must match with one of the actors in the second column.

> **TIP:** There are two ways to make a movie "Match 'Em Up" puzzle more challenging:
>
> 1. Include actors who people may forget were in the movies you have selected.

2. Include actors who have been in more than one of your selected movies.

(Similarly, for sports, you might list athletes in one column and their matching teams in the other, but to make it more challenging, you could include lesser-known players of a sport and/or players who have played on more than one of the teams in the other column.)

GAME TIME (MOVIES AND ACTORS)

Show the game board to the teams in your group at the same time. The first team to figure out all twenty matches wins.

SAMPLE PUZZLE (ANSWERS IN THE BACK)

MOVIES		ACTORS	
1.	A Few Good Men	**A.**	Paul Giamatti
2.	Bruce Almighty	**B.**	Matt Dillon
3.	Horrible Bosses	**C.**	Meg Ryan
4.	The Dark Knight Rises	**D.**	Gene Hackman
5.	Pulp Fiction	**E.**	Kelly Lynch
6.	Unforgiven	**F.**	Kevin Bacon
7.	Cocktail	**G.**	Eddie Murphy
8.	Shrek	**H.**	Charlize Theron
9.	The Mask	**I.**	Jennifer Aniston
10.	Beverly Hills Cop	**J.**	Tom Cruise
11.	Driving Miss Daisy	**K.**	Steve Carell
12.	Get Shorty	**L.**	Jason Alexander
13.	Top Gun	**M.**	Anne Hathaway
14.	Trading Places	**N.**	Julia Roberts
15.	Cider House Rules	**O.**	Morgan Freeman
16.	There's Something About Mary	**P.**	Cameron Diaz
17.	Pretty Woman	**Q.**	Judge Reinhold
18.	Steel Magnolias	**R.**	Jim Carrey
19.	The Color of Money	**S.**	Bruce Willis
20.	Saving Private Ryan	**T.**	Dan Aykroyd

TRIPLETS

FIND ALL THE GROUPS OF THREE IN A CROWDED LIST!

PREPARATION

Make a "Triplets" puzzle by creating fifteen groups of three related words. For example, one group of related words might be *bat, diamond*, and *glove* (things related to baseball). Another group might be *basketball, football*, and *rainfall* (words that end with *-all*). Another group might be *mitten, hat*, and *sneaker* (things you wear). Yet another group might be *cat, rat*, and *fat* (words that rhyme).

These examples might seem easy to match up. However, when mixed together, the groupings aren't as obvious. (For example, there's a good chance a player may want to put *hat* with *cat* and *rat* or *glove* with *mitten* and *hat*.)

This puzzle should be hard enough that players have to think about the different combinations and why certain words may go together. Players may create combinations that simply require some thought, but they might also include words in each three-word group that could fit into several combinations.

NOTE: This puzzle may take longer to create than others, depending upon how complex you wish to make it. You can certainly make it easier for yourself and the other players by using fewer than fifteen groups and simpler combinations.

Once the player creating the game board has all fifteen groups, he or she mixes all of the words into a master list of forty-five words.

GAME TIME

Players must find the fifteen triplet groups within the master list.

SAMPLE PUZZLE (ANSWERS IN THE BACK)

LIVED
JACKSON
CRANIUM
CHALET
RACKET
KAYAK
YALE
ROW
CLEATS
SOPRANO
WHEAT
FRENCH
BATTLESHIP
SPLASH
SCRUPLES

DECAL
BOA
WOW
SKINNY
GARTER
HELMET
TUDOR
SAIL
MADISON
ADAGIO
SALINGER
SKATEBOARD
JAZZ
RICE
RANCH

SKYSCRAPER
COLUMBIA
FLOW
CREOLE
STEINBECK
BUTTER
RYE
SUPERDOME
VIPER
RATTLESNAKE
FITZGERALD
WILSON
CRESCENDO
TABOO
STATS

CHOPPED-UP CELEBRITIES

JUST PUT ALL OF THE PEOPLE BACK TOGETHER—SIMPLE AS THAT!

PREPARATION

Draw a grid with six rows and six columns for a total of thirty-six boxes. Think of nine names (first and last) of well-known people, and make sure the first and last names are a combined eight letters or more. Write the names on slips of paper, then chop up each name into four pieces of at least two letters each. For example, the name *Oprah Winfrey* "chopped up" could have the following pieces:

1. OP
2. RAH
3. WIN
4. FREY

The name *Quentin Tarantino* chopped up could be:

1. QU
2. ENTI

3. NTARA
4. NTINO

Now take all of the thirty-six chopped-up pieces of all nine names and place them randomly in the thirty-six different squares in the grid.

GAME TIME

Players from each team must match up the pieces and figure out the nine famous people. The first team to put all the pieces back together, figuratively speaking, wins!

> **TIP:** Nine names can be difficult, so you may want to start with four names using a grid of four rows and four columns with a total of sixteen boxes. Then graduate to the bigger grid!

SAMPLE PUZZLE (ANSWERS IN THE BACK)

ARLI	AGG	BRO	STRO	INST	TON
OMI	EIN	ZETHE	PLA	ER	NAJO
NJA	AN	ERTE	NG	RON	LLC
JO	BI	CIDOD	YDE	LARM	MES
ALB	HNN	LE	MI	PP	NGO
CH	NEI	GELI	LIN	CKJ	LIE

FIND THE CONNECTION

ALLOW ME TO INTRODUCE YOU TO THE SISTER YOU NEVER KNEW.

PREPARATION

This puzzle involves finding two words that have a special connection. For example, *conditioner* and *hockey* may not seem related, but both have a connection to the word *air*: *air hockey* and *air conditioner. Butter* and *allergy* both have a connection to *peanut*: *peanut butter* and *peanut allergy. Arrest* and *doll* have a connection to *house*: *house arrest* and *dollhouse*.

NOTE: When a word is combined with a "connector" (a connecting word like *air, peanut*, and *house* in the example above) those two words can be in any order (e.g., *cell phone* and *phone book*, with *phone* as the connector). Additionally, it doesn't matter if the words, when connected, become one word (*eyelash*) or two (*black eye*).

To create this puzzle, players come up with twenty groups of two words that each have a "connector" and compile those forty words into one long, randomly ordered list on the page.

GAME TIME

With the game board set, players attempt to find the twenty groups and list the connector next to each group.

IMPORTANT: Many players find these puzzles extremely difficult (even when working as a team) if the words in the group of forty present many possible matching combinations with many different connectors. To make it challenging but still possible to complete in a reasonable amount of time, players should present a list of twenty-five connectors—twenty of which are the REAL connectors for the puzzle, with the other five just to throw people off.

All the players on each team must figure out which twenty are the real connectors and where they belong.

SAMPLE PUZZLE (ANSWERS IN THE BACK)

BUNNY
PINKY
SUPER
LACE
PLACE
FLY
NEWS
POLICE
ROPE
BIRTHDAY
SEAT
WAX
PLANNER
CEILING

GLASSES
PUDDING
WAVE
WHITE
SUN
BUS
HORSE
SKI
LAKES
HOLE
HORN
ENGINE
BROADWAY
SPURT

SET
HORMONE
PLATE
BASEBALL
BALL
PRIVATE
SWITCH
INFECTION
BICYCLE
PAPER
SPREE
IDENTICAL

HINT: Here are the twenty actual connectors for this puzzle, plus 5 which don't belong! Which are the real connectors, and where do they go? Match each of the twenty with a pair from above:

RABBIT, EAR, SUN, TREE, FINGER, HAPPY, TOILET, GLOVE, GROWTH, PARTY, JUMP, RACE, BREAD, SCHOOL, LIGHT, PAPER, BULLETIN, MAN, FAN, INVESTIGATOR, CRIME, SHOE, PLAY, FIRE, TWIN

WHAT'S MISSING?

FILL IN THE BLANKS WITH THE RIGHT GROUP OF LETTERS.

PREPARATION

Separate a sheet of paper into two columns with a line or fold. Make a numbered list from 1 to 10 on the left side of the paper, leaving plenty of room to the right of each number. In the column on the right, make a lettered list from A to J.

Next, come up with ten random words. Each word should be at least six letters long. In the list on the left, draw dashes next to each number representing the letters in each word. Write in the words over the dashes, but leave out FOUR LETTERS of each word. Keep each set of the four missing letters together (in any order) and place them in the lettered list in the right-hand column.

TIP: Don't necessarily write the four missing letters directly across from their matching words. Mix them up by placing each group in a different row.

GAME TIME

The first team to figure out all of the words in the left column wins!

SAMPLE PUZZLE (ANSWERS IN THE BACK)

1.	B_T_E_F_Y	**A.**	PLEO
2.	_H_W_ _	**B.**	REOF
3.	_ _A_PO_	**C.**	URLT
4.	FO_ _ _A_L	**D.**	YAER
5.	_O_D_ _	**E.**	ATHC
6.	_L_IM_ _E	**F.**	HOSM
7.	_RC_I_E_T	**G.**	LIYH
8.	G_ _M_N_	**H.**	ERSO
9.	P_ O _ _SS_R	**I.**	OTLB
10.	_O_ _ DA_	**J.**	UATT

ANSWERS

MOVIE MATCH

1F
2K
3I
4M
5S
6O
7E
8P
9R
10Q
11T
12D
13C
14G
15H
16B
17L
18N
19J
20A

TRIPLETS

1. A. LIVED; B. DECAL; C. FLOW (Words backward & forward)
2. A. SKYSCRAPER; B. SKATEBOARD; C. SKINNY (Sk- words)
3. A. KAYAK; B. WOW; C. STATS (Palindromes)
4. A. BOA; B. GARTER; C. VIPER (Snakes)
5. A. CREOLE; B. JAZZ; C. SUPERDOME (New Orleans)
6. A. RICE; B. COLUMBIA; C. YALE (Universities)
7. A. WHEAT; B. RYE; C. FRENCH (Bread)
8. A. FITZGERALD; B. STEINBECK; C. SALINGER (Authors)
9. A. TABOO; B. SCRUPLES; C. CRANIUM (Board games)
10. A. TUDOR; B. RANCH; C. CHALET (Houses)

11. A. JACKSON; B. WILSON; C. MADISON (Presidents)
12. A. HELMET; B. RACKET; C. CLEATS (To do with sports)
13. A. BATTLESHIP; B. BUTTER; C. RATTLESNAKE (Words with TT)
14. A. ROW; B. SPLASH; C. SAIL (In water)
15. A. SOPRANO; B. ADAGIO; C. CRESCENDO (Music terms)

CHOPPED-UP CELEBRITIES

1. JOHNNY DEPP
2. ANGELINA JOLIE
3. CHARLIZE THERON
4. NEIL ARMSTRONG
5. BILL CLINTON
6. PLACIDO DOMINGO
7. MICK JAGGER
8. LEBRON JAMES
9. ALBERT EINSTEIN

FIND THE CONNECTION

1. BUNNY & HOLE (RABBIT)
2. INFECTION & WAX (EAR)
3. GLASSES & SET (SUN)
4. PINKY & LAKES (FINGER)
5. PAPER & SEAT (TOILET)
6. SPURT & HORMONE (GROWTH)

7. PLANNER & BIRTHDAY (PARTY)
8. ROPE & SKI (JUMP)
9. BICYCLE & HORSE (RACE)
10. WHITE & PUDDING (BREAD)
11. BUS & PRIVATE (SCHOOL)
12. SWITCH & SUN (LIGHT)
13. NEWS & PLATE (PAPER)
14. POLICE & SUPER (MAN)
15. CEILING & BASEBALL (FAN)
16. SPREE & WAVE (CRIME)
17. HORN & LACE (SHOE)
18. BROADWAY & BALL (PLAY)
19. PLACE & FLY (FIRE)
20. IDENTICAL & ENGINE (TWIN)

Not connectors in the puzzle: TREE, BULLETIN, INVESTIGATOR, HAPPY, and GLOVE.

WHAT'S MISSING?

1C: BUTTERFLY
2H: SHOWER
3F: SHAMPOO
4I: FOOTBALL
5A: POODLE
6J: ULTIMATE
7E: ARCHITECT
8D: GERMANY
9B: PROFESSOR
10G: HOLIDAY

THANK YOU! THANK YOU! THANK YOU!

. . . to Taylor, Rebekah, Lesly, Barbara, Jerry, Graham, Ridley, Lindsay, Brian, Michael, Meri, Greta, Eva, Rocky, Lisa, Levon, Kelly, Anthony C., Jimmy, Jud, Marvin, Rose, Debbie, Louis, Danny, Cynthia, Jennifer, Mike, Anthony P., Richie, David, Jill, Abe, Georgia, Kevin, Devin, Phil, Megan, Matt, Danielle, Nadia, Joe, Rachel, Greg, Russell, Bob, Jean, Emily, Chip, Shane . . . and many more in my never-ending focus group who have volunteered through the years to have some fun and make this book possible.

ABOUT THE AUTHOR

BRAD BERGER grew up in Great Neck, New York. He attended the University of Colorado, where he earned a degree in French, Italian, and German and spent several years living and working in Europe. He currently resides on Long Island, where he works as president and publisher of a 130-year-old, family-owned publishing company.

Since his childhood, Brad has enjoyed bringing his friends and family together to play all kinds of games. However, with the invention of so much technology, Brad saw a decline in group-based activities within his own family and circle of friends. Inspired to bring people back together without technological interruption, Brad crafted the ultimate playbook of new games to give people a reason to come together and "unplug" for a while.

Website: www.bradbergergames.com

ABOUT FAMILIUS

Welcome to a place where books—and family—are beautiful. Familius: a book publisher dedicated to helping families be happy. If you feel a few friends and family might benefit from what you've read, let us know and we'll be happy to provide you with quantity discounts. Simply email us at specialorders@familius.com.

Website: www.familius.com
Facebook: www.facebook.com/paterfamilius
Twitter: @familiustalk, @paterfamilius1
Pinterest: www.pinterest.com/familius